Eyewitness
Evolution

Snails with feelers extended

Skull of early hominid *Homo erectus*

Rock containing fossilized remains of several species of trilobite

Duck-billed platypus

Fossilized skeleton of *Procynosuchus*, a mammal-like reptile

Skull of modern human

Rock composed of millions of sea-shells

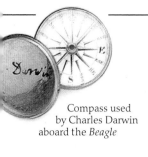

Compass used
by Charles Darwin
aboard the *Beagle*

Butterfly wing from
Charles Darwin's collection

Eyewitness
Evolution

Written by
LINDA GAMLIN

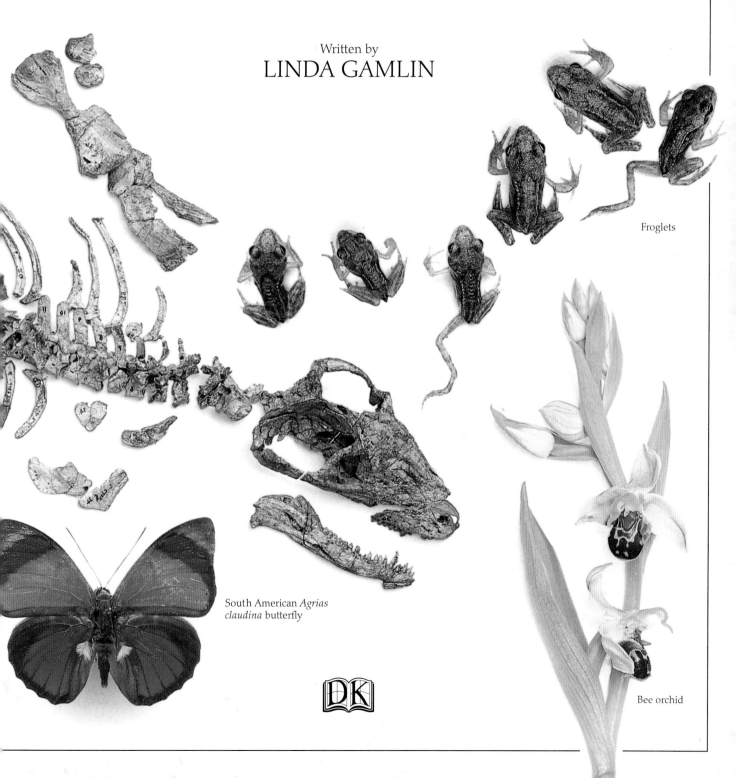

Froglets

South American *Agrias
claudina* butterfly

Bee orchid

DK

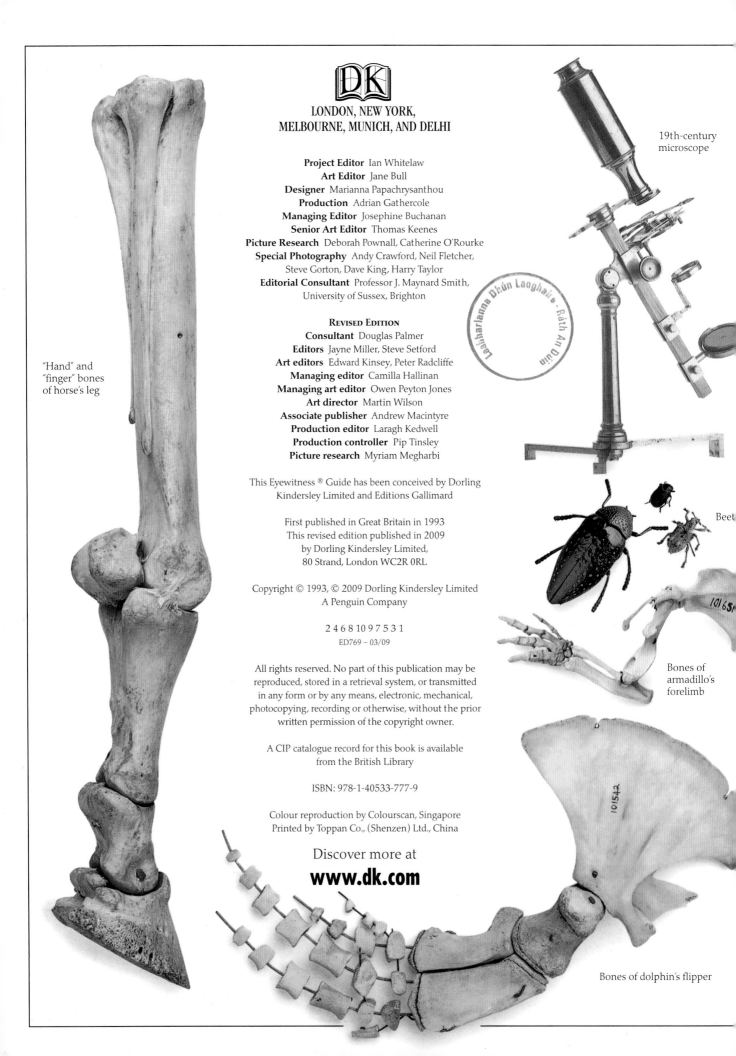

"Hand" and
"finger" bones
of horse's leg

19th-century
microscope

Beet

Bones of
armadillo's
forelimb

Bones of dolphin's flipper

DK

LONDON, NEW YORK,
MELBOURNE, MUNICH, AND DELHI

Project Editor Ian Whitelaw
Art Editor Jane Bull
Designer Marianna Papachrysanthou
Production Adrian Gathercole
Managing Editor Josephine Buchanan
Senior Art Editor Thomas Keenes
Picture Research Deborah Pownall, Catherine O'Rourke
Special Photography Andy Crawford, Neil Fletcher,
Steve Gorton, Dave King, Harry Taylor
Editorial Consultant Professor J. Maynard Smith,
University of Sussex, Brighton

REVISED EDITION
Consultant Douglas Palmer
Editors Jayne Miller, Steve Setford
Art editors Edward Kinsey, Peter Radcliffe
Managing editor Camilla Hallinan
Managing art editor Owen Peyton Jones
Art director Martin Wilson
Associate publisher Andrew Macintyre
Production editor Laragh Kedwell
Production controller Pip Tinsley
Picture research Myriam Megharbi

This Eyewitness ® Guide has been conceived by Dorling
Kindersley Limited and Editions Gallimard

First published in Great Britain in 1993
This revised edition published in 2009
by Dorling Kindersley Limited,
80 Strand, London WC2R 0RL

A CIP catalogue record for this book is available
from the British Library

ISBN: 978-1-40533-777-9

Colour reproduction by Colourscan, Singapore
Printed by Toppan Co., (Shenzen) Ltd., China

Discover more at
www.dk.com

Contents

Members of the
insect order Hemiptera

Creation stories

WHERE DO PEOPLE COME FROM? How did the world begin? Where do plants and animals come from? People have been thinking about these questions for thousands of years, and there are many answers in the form of traditional stories. Some of these stories tell of a god who created the world and everything in it, including people. Other stories have many gods, who each made different things and then fought great battles for control of the world. Not all stories describe the world as having been created, however. Some tell of the world growing out of nothing, or out of chaos, without any creator. According to Buddhist beliefs, there was no beginning: instead, the Universe goes through endless cycles of being and non-being. The stories are all very different, but they often try to explain certain things about life. Some explain why people get ill and die, or why there is night and day. They may also explain some minor features of living things, such as why snakes have no legs. More importantly, the stories often give people rules or guidelines for their lives. They may say something about the different ways in which men and women should behave, or how people should treat the animals and plants around them. Many religious authorities regard these stories as valuable lessons on how people should live, rather than factual accounts of how life on Earth actually began.

CREATORS OF THE WORLD
The Japanese creation story tells th
in the beginning there were eight
gods. When the youngest two,
Izanagi and Izanami, stirred the
ocean with a jewelled spear, falling
drops of water formed an
island. They came to live
there and Izanami
gave birth to all
the islands
of Japan.

IN THE BEGINNING
These 16th-century illustrations show the Biblical creation story, which Christians and Jews share. There are two versions of the story, both in the first book of the Bible, Genesis. In the first version, shown here, man and woman are made simultaneously on the sixth day of creation. In the second version of the story, God creates the first man, Adam, before any other living thing. He then plants the Garden of Eden and makes all the animals. His final act is to create the first woman, Eve.

Egg

HATCHED FROM AN EGG
This carving of a bird-headed god holding an egg comes from Easter Island in the Pacific Ocean. Here tradition says that the first people hatched from eggs laid by birds. On other Pacific islands, people were said to have hatched from turtles' eggs, or from rocks.

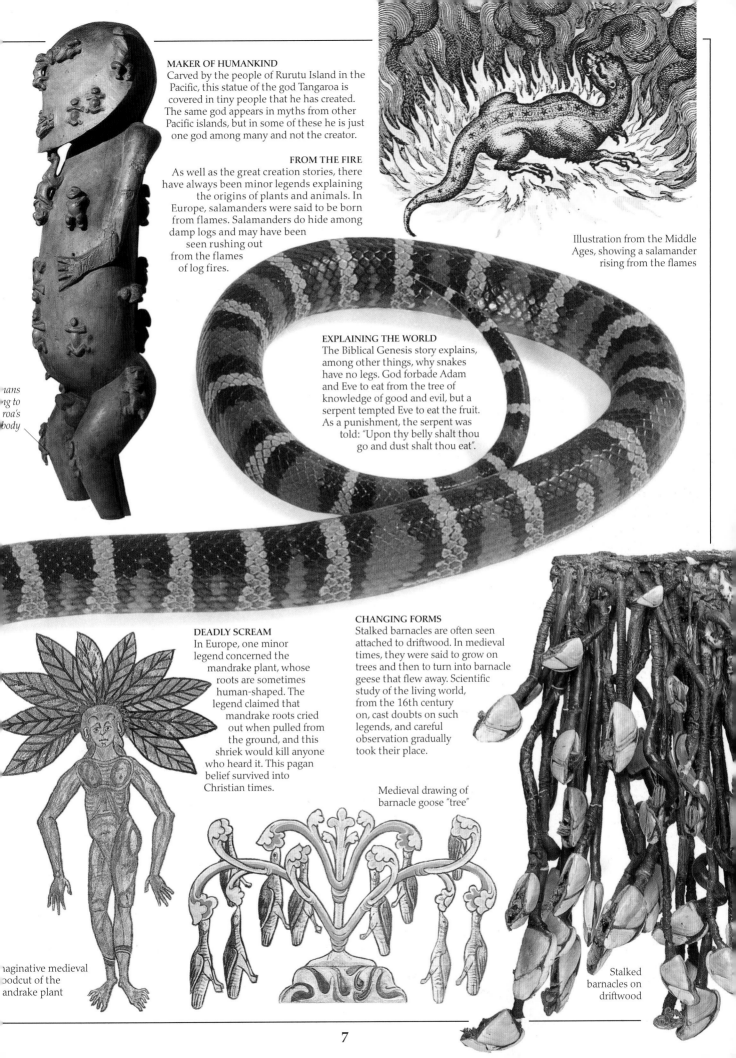

MAKER OF HUMANKIND
Carved by the people of Rurutu Island in the Pacific, this statue of the god Tangaroa is covered in tiny people that he has created. The same god appears in myths from other Pacific islands, but in some of these he is just one god among many and not the creator.

FROM THE FIRE
As well as the great creation stories, there have always been minor legends explaining the origins of plants and animals. In Europe, salamanders were said to be born from flames. Salamanders do hide among damp logs and may have been seen rushing out from the flames of log fires.

Illustration from the Middle Ages, showing a salamander rising from the flames

mans ng to roa's body

EXPLAINING THE WORLD
The Biblical Genesis story explains, among other things, why snakes have no legs. God forbade Adam and Eve to eat from the tree of knowledge of good and evil, but a serpent tempted Eve to eat the fruit. As a punishment, the serpent was told: "Upon thy belly shalt thou go and dust shalt thou eat".

DEADLY SCREAM
In Europe, one minor legend concerned the mandrake plant, whose roots are sometimes human-shaped. The legend claimed that mandrake roots cried out when pulled from the ground, and this shriek would kill anyone who heard it. This pagan belief survived into Christian times.

CHANGING FORMS
Stalked barnacles are often seen attached to driftwood. In medieval times, they were said to grow on trees and then to turn into barnacle geese that flew away. Scientific study of the living world, from the 16th century on, cast doubts on such legends, and careful observation gradually took their place.

Medieval drawing of barnacle goose "tree"

maginative medieval oodcut of the andrake plant

Stalked barnacles on driftwood

Fossils and fairytales

TAB.VII
1
chap: 5.
ſ. 142.

FOSSILS ARE THE REMAINS or impressions of living things hardened in rock. People have been finding fossils for at least 30,000 years. Ice Age hunters made them into necklaces, and the idea that fossils had magical properties may well have begun then. Magical beliefs about fossils became common all over the world. The Chinese kept tiny fossilized fish in their food stores to keep away insect pests called silverfish. The Roman scholar Pliny the Elder wrote that fossilized sea urchins could cure snake-bites and ensure success in battle. He also collected some extraordinary "tall tales" to explain the origins of fossils: sea urchin fossils were said to be formed from balls of foam created by masses of entwined snakes. Other people developed theories to explain fossils in general. One idea was that the rain picked up the seeds and eggs of living things from the sea. When the rain fell and seeped into rocks, the seeds and eggs grew into stony replicas of their true selves. This was an attempt to explain why so many fossils are clearly sea creatures.

A more fanciful theory, popular from medieval times until the 17th century, was that Earth had its own "creative force", or *vis plastica*, and this force was trying to make copies of living things.

ELFIN FARE
Thinking they were fairy loaves, people in southern England kept fossil heart urchins like this in their larders to ensure that there would always be bread for the family.

Dr Pl[...]
horse-l[...]
illustrati[...]
of the fos[...]

STONE HORSES
This unusual fossil is the cast, or mould, of the inside of a shell called *Myophorella*. The shell itself has dissolved away. The living animal was similar to an oyster, having two shells hel[...] together by a strong muscle. This left a circular mark on each side, and Dr Robert Plot (1640–1696) interpreted these as eyes. With great imagination, he also saw two ears and a mane and declared that this was an attempt by Earth's *vis plastica* to make a horse's head.

Fossil mould

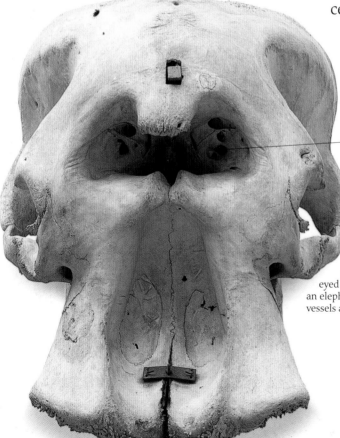

Opening in skull for trunk

ONE-EYED MAN
When skulls like this were found in fossil form on the Mediterranean island of Sicily, the ancient Greeks imagined giant men, each with a single eye in his forehead. This belief gave rise to the legend of the one-eyed Cyclops. In fact, this is the skull of an elephant, and the hole is where its blood vessels and airways ran down to the trunk.

BLINDING THE GIANT
On a vase from ancient Greece, the hero Odysseus is shown blinding the Cyclops Polyphemus with an iron brand as he sleeps in his cave on Mount Aetna in Sicily. Odysseus and his companions were able to escape from the island but made an enemy of Poseidon the sea god, the father of the Cyclops.

Fossilized sharks' teeth

Root

Cutting edge

TONGUES FROM THE SKY
Pliny the Elder believed that these fossils were stone tongues that fell to Earth during eclipses of the moon. In 1667 Niels Stensen dissected a dead shark and realized that they were simply sharks' teeth. He was not the first with a sensible explanation for fossils, but most people preferred the tall stories.

THICAL MONSTERS
ring the last ice age 40,000 years ago, there
e giant bears in Europe. Some died in
es while hibernating, and many were
silized because the cool dark cave
rironment helped preserve their
letal remains along with
tprints and claw marks.
en the skulls of these
rs, with their huge
ine teeth, were
nd in the Middle
es, they were
ught to
ong to fire-
athing
agons".

Cave bear skull

Drawing of ammonite

SERPENTS OF STONE
In northern England the coiled fossils of ancient ammonites, sea animals like the living *Nautilus*, were once thought to be snakes that had been turned to stone by a saint. Local people even carved heads on to these "snake stones", just to prove the point.

Grinding teeth

Canine tooth

Carved snake's head

thical
nged dragon

FOSSIL FUNGUS?
Despite its toadstool-like appearance, this strange object is actually a sponge from an ancient sea. The sponge has become fossilized in flint. Toadstools are too soft to become fossilized, but are rarely preserved in amber.

Fossil ammonite

Victims of the flood

O**NE OF THE GREATEST PUZZLES** about fossils was the appearance of shells and other sea creatures high up on mountain tops. Some Ancient Greek scholars, such as Pythagoras and Herodotus, reasoned that such mountain rocks must once have been under the sea, but the early Christian philosopher Tertullian (around 155–222 CE) claimed that the waters of the flood, as described in the Bible, had carried shells up to this height. This idea was considered by Leonardo da Vinci (1452–1519), who made careful observations of fossils and calculated what would happen during a massive flood. He concluded that the explanation made no sense. Despite Leonardo's efforts, the idea was popular among geologists until the late 18th century. By then the theo was known as diluvialism. It proposed that all Earth's sedimentary rock (made of sand, mud, and lime) had been deposited by floods when all the victims had been drowned and preserved as fossils within them. As a popular notion, rather than a scientific theory, it survived amongst fundamentalists into the 19th centu but by 1820 the evidence against it was so strong that the idea had largely disappeared.

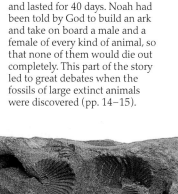

NOAH AND THE FLOOD
The Bible describes an immense flood that covered all Earth's land and lasted for 40 days. Noah had been told by God to build an ark and take on board a male and a female of every kind of animal, so that none of them would die out completely. This part of the story led to great debates when the fossils of large extinct animals were discovered (pp. 14–15).

Shelly rock from the top of Mount Snowdon in Wales

FOSSIL HUNTER
Johann Scheuzer (1672–1733), a Swiss fossil collector, was an enthusiastic "diluvialist" – one who believed that the flood had created all sedimentary rocks and fossils. He described one of his finds as "the bony skeleton of one of those infamous men whose sins brought upon the world the dire misfortune of the deluge". It was a fossil of a giant salamander.

RAISING THE ROCKS
During the 18th and 19th centuries, geologists began to understand how sea shells could appear on mountain tops. They realized that most sedimentary rocks had been deposited in the sea as sand, mud, and lime. Here the remains of dead organisms were buried and fossilized as the sediment turned to rock. Later Earth movements squeezed and broke the rocks, buckling them into folds, so that rocks that had been under the sea were raised into mountains.

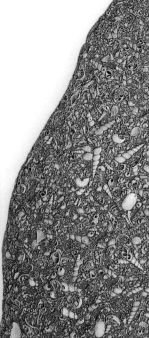

...he missing fossils

...l fossils were creatures killed by
...flood, there would be fossils of a
...t many land animals that were
...wned as the waters rose, but few
...ils of fish, since they could swim.
...act, the opposite is true. Seafloor
...tures are some of the most
...mon fossils, while land animals
...relatively rare. However, land
...ironments such as swamps
... lakes, and their life are
...etimes fossilized.

Lizard

...ELY FOSSILIZED
...le fossils of
...ed dwelling
...tures such as
...s and snails are
...n found, insects,
...ds, and marine
...le stars are rare.

...LY ROCK
...e rocks are made
...rely of rapidly
...osited shells.
...thers, like coal and
... chalk, built up
... very slowly.

Rare fossil of an insect

Uncommon
dragonfly
fossil

Fossilized
brittle star,
a marine
animal

Fossil perch

Chalk and coal

As people learned more about
sedimentary rocks, it became
clear that these cannot all have
been laid down in a few years.
Chalk and coal for example
are made up of the remains
of living things – trillions of
microscopic shells, in the case
of chalk, and thousands of
plant remains piled one upon
another, for coal. Clearly, such
rocks must have taken a very
long time to build up.

ROCK OF AGES
In 1858 a geologist, looking at chalk
under the microscope, found that
it was almost entirely made
up of tiny shells. These
shells belonged to
microscopic creatures
that floated at the
ocean's surface. We
know this because their
relatives still do so
today. Chalk cliffs
(above) show how thick
the layers of chalk are.

MICROSCOPIC STRUCTURE
When chalk is imaged under an
electron microscope, its structure
reveals that it is made up almost
entirely of the calcareous
(calcium-rich) skeletons
of minute creatures.

Fern fossil
in coal

THE COAL FORESTS
Coal is made almost entirely of plant
remains from bogs and swampy
forests. When the plants died, their
tissues did not rot away but gradually
turned into peat. This was then
compressed by the growing weight
above it, turning it into coal. Coal
seams can be 20 m (66 ft) thick.

Jean-Baptiste de Lamarck

J EAN-BAPTISTE DE LAMARCK (1744–1829) was one of the first people
propose a theory of evolution. He believed that there were two
evolutionary forces at work. The first was a "tendency to progression", a
automatic process by which all living things became more complex. The
second force was the need to fit in with the local environment: as
animals tried to fit in, their efforts produced a bodily change. In this wa
the giraffe developed a long neck by stretching for the leaves of trees,
and wading birds grew long legs by straining upwards to keep
themselves dry. These two forces were not in harmony, according
to Lamarck. The first force working alone
would produce perfect patterns of
increasing complexity among animals,
but the second force interfered with the first. For the second
force to work, characteristics acquired by the parents (such as a longer
neck) would have to be passed on to their offspring. This is now
known not to happen, except in a few rare cases, but in Lamarck's day it
was a common idea. For a century afterwards, everyone, including Darwin
(p. 20), believed it to be true. Today, the term "Lamarckism" is often used
just to mean the inheritance of acquired characteristics. The other
parts of Lamarck's theory have largely been forgotten.

REVOLUTIONARY THINKER
French naturalist
Lamarck made people
think about evolution.

HIGH AND I
According to Lamarck's theory
trying to keep its belly out of
water a wading bird "acquires
habit of stretching and elonga
its legs". In this way, he belie
species such as this purple he
developed their long l

Subtle fluids

Lamarck suggested that there were "subtle fluids"
flowing all around a body and all through it, and
that these produced both movement and change.
He regarded the fluids as mysterious, but believed
he could identify two: caloric (heat) and electricity.

CHARGED IDEAS
Lamarck believed that his "subtle fluids" were involved in both
kinds of change – the "tendency to progression" and the striving
to fit local conditions. Electricity was of great interest to scientists
at the time, and it appealed to Lamarck because it could be felt
but not seen. The French scientist Jean-Antoine Nollet
(1700–1770) set up experiments (right) to study the effects
of static electricity on
plants and animals.

FEELING THE WAY FORWARD
Lamarck used snails as an exam
of how "subtle fluids" worked.
Snails have poor vision, and he
imagined an ancestral snail with
no feelers, groping about with it
head. Its efforts to feel the way
would send "masses of
nervous fluid as well as
other liquids" to the
front of the head.
In time this
would produce
"eye-tipped
tentacles".

Extended feelers

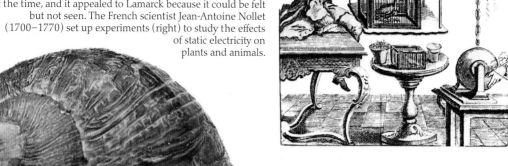

ooking at the evidence

upport his claim that evolution had rred, Lamarck pointed to the way t members of a species, such as a terfly species, can vary from place to e. His ideas about the inheritance of uired characteristics and about the tinuous creation of simple life forms re later proven to be false.

Agrias claudina sardanapalus
Peru and Brazil

Agrias claudina claudina
Eastern Central Brazil

Agrias claudina lugens
Peru

SPONTANEOUS LIFE
If all living things are progressing, why are there still simple creatures left? Lamarck believed that new ones arose by "spontaneous generation" of microscopic life from non-living matter, such as wet straw. French microbiologist Louis Pasteur (1822–1895) showed this to be an illusion. If the straw was boiled thoroughly, no living things developed.

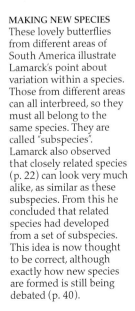
Agrias claudina claudianus
Southeastern Brazil

PASSING IT ON
If acquired characteristics were inherited, as Lamarck thought, then the children of white-skinned people living in hot countries would be born with sun-tanned skins. This English family in 19th-century India shows that they are not.

MAKING NEW SPECIES
These lovely butterflies from different areas of South America illustrate Lamarck's point about variation within a species. Those from different areas can all interbreed, so they must all belong to the same species. They are called "subspecies". Lamarck also observed that closely related species (p. 22) can look very much alike, as similar as these subspecies. From this he concluded that related species had developed from a set of subspecies. This idea is now thought to be correct, although exactly how new species are formed is still being debated (p. 40).

Agrias claudina godmani
Central Brazil

POET AND BOTANIST
Even before Lamarck, the poet Johann Goethe (1749–1832) had published evolutionary ideas about plants.

Agrias claudina intermedius
Southeastern Colombia, Venezuela

Extinct animals

ACCORDING TO THE BIBLE, Noah took two of every kind of animal into his ark, and all survived the Flood. Christianity also taught that each living thing was an essential link in God's chain of creation. Thus it would be impossible for any of them to have died out completely, or become "extinct". When fossils of unknown creatures were found, it was assumed that the animals were still living somewhere in the world. However, by the end of the 18th century, the fossils of such gigantic creatures had been found that this explanation began to seem unlikely. In North America the massive bones of the giant ground sloth and the mastodon were discovered. No unexplored regions were large enough to hide such giants, and the suspicion that they had become extinct began to grow. French scientists, less influenced by religious views following the upheavals of the French Revolution, were among the first to accept the idea of extinction. Afterwards, the idea was accepted in the US, and then, more slowly, in other countries.

LOST WORLDS
The strange duck-billed platypus of Australia was only discovered by western science in 1799. Discoveries like this suggested that there were many unknown creatures in the world and that "extinct" animals could still be alive somewhere.

HARD TO HIDE
This is a cross-section, shown half life-size, through the upper molar teeth of a giant ground sloth, known as *Megatherium*. The fossils of another ground sloth, almost as large, were found in North America and first described by Thomas Jefferson in 1797. A living animal of this size could clearly not remain undiscovered, unlike small animals such as the platypus. By the 1830s the idea of extinction had become widely accepted.

Giant ground sloth skeleton

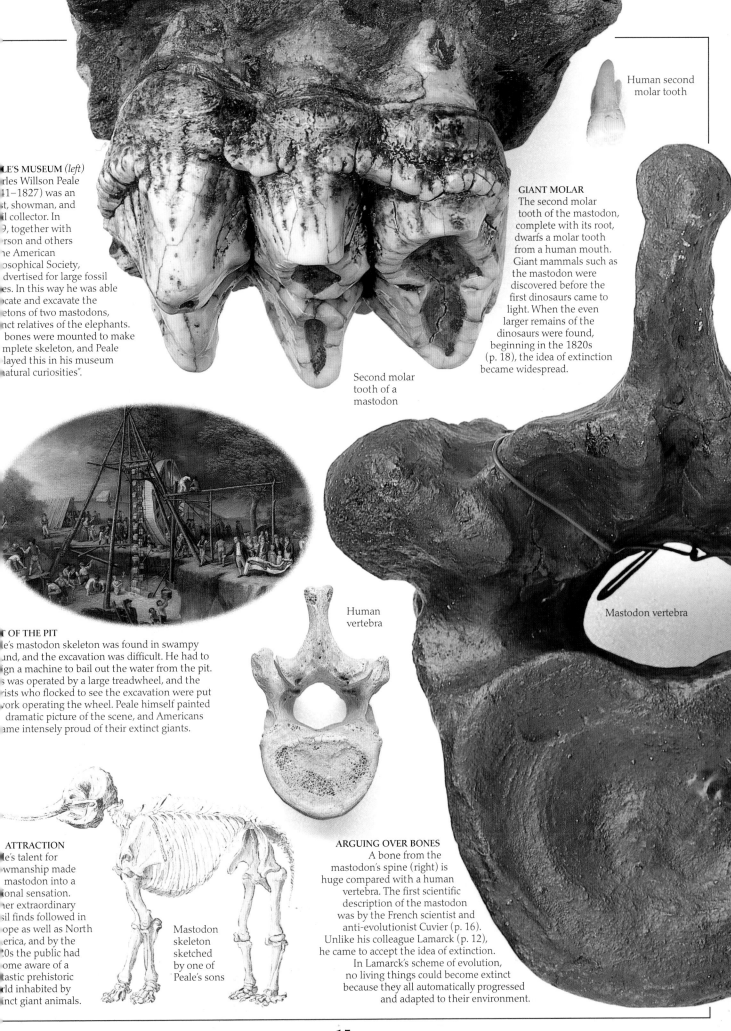

Human second
molar tooth

GIANT MOLAR
The second molar
tooth of the mastodon,
complete with its root,
dwarfs a molar tooth
from a human mouth.
Giant mammals such as
the mastodon were
discovered before the
first dinosaurs came to
light. When the even
larger remains of the
dinosaurs were found,
beginning in the 1820s
(p. 18), the idea of extinction
became widespread.

Second molar
tooth of a
mastodon

LE'S MUSEUM *(left)*
rles Willson Peale
1–1827) was an
t, showman, and
l collector. In
9, together with
rson and others
e American
osophical Society,
dvertised for large fossil
es. In this way he was able
cate and excavate the
etons of two mastodons,
nct relatives of the elephants.
bones were mounted to make
mplete skeleton, and Peale
layed this in his museum
atural curiosities".

Mastodon vertebra

Human
vertebra

T OF THE PIT
e's mastodon skeleton was found in swampy
nd, and the excavation was difficult. He had to
ign a machine to bail out the water from the pit.
s was operated by a large treadwheel, and the
rists who flocked to see the excavation were put
ork operating the wheel. Peale himself painted
dramatic picture of the scene, and Americans
ame intensely proud of their extinct giants.

ATTRACTION
le's talent for
wmanship made
mastodon into a
ional sensation.
er extraordinary
sil finds followed in
ope as well as North
erica, and by the
0s the public had
ome aware of a
tastic prehistoric
ld inhabited by
nct giant animals.

Mastodon
skeleton
sketched
by one of
Peale's sons

ARGUING OVER BONES
A bone from the
mastodon's spine (right) is
huge compared with a human
vertebra. The first scientific
description of the mastodon
was by the French scientist and
anti-evolutionist Cuvier (p. 16).
Unlike his colleague Lamarck (p. 12),
he came to accept the idea of extinction.
In Lamarck's scheme of evolution,
no living things could become extinct
because they all automatically progressed
and adapted to their environment.

A series of catastrophes

Industrial expansion in the 18th century created a need for iron ore and coal, as well as canals for transport. Mines and excavations went deep underground, which led to great advances in geology. By the late 18th century the German naturalist Abraham Werner (1750–1817) had divided rock strata into three groups – Primary, Secondary, and Tertiary, from oldest to youngest. Werner thought that all these strata had been laid down by a series of catastrophic worldwide floods. By the beginning of the 19th century, it was realized independently by William Smith (1769–1839) in England and Georges Cuvier (1769–1832) in France that fossils could be used to characterize successive strata. Cuvier also thought that successive strata resulted from a series of catastrophic floods. Nevertheless, fossils were shown to be particularly useful for subdividing rock strata and mapping their distribution for the first time. By the mid 19th century, geologists such as Charles Lyell (1797–1875) were arguing that sedimentary rock strata were not laid down by catastrophic events but rather by everyday, gradual processes of erosion and depostion. The subdivision of geological strata and time was refined by many European geologists into a series of geological periods such as the Carboniferous and Jurassic (p. 28).

GEORGES CUVIER
Cuvier believed that catastrophes had stripped much of Earth of life several times, but that some regions had always escaped, and animals had spread again from those regions. Later he also accepted that some animals had become extinct, while Lamarck refused to believe this. Cuvier was against evolution, believing that life had "stood still" between catastrophes. Lamarck and Cuvier became life-long enemies.

EVIDENCE FROM EGYPT
Napoleon's troops invaded Egypt in 1798 and brought back mummies found in the pyramids. Among these was a mummified ibis, and Cuvier was jubilant to find that its skeleton was the same as that of a living ibis. He claimed this absence of change as evidence that Lamarck was wrong and that evolution did not occur.

UNCHANGED IBIS
The modern ibis is indeed the same as that of Ancient Egy Some species do stay much same for thousands, or eve millions, of years, while other species can evolve very rapidly. It all deper on the circumstances. Lamarck and Cuvier w each right on one poir and wrong on another Lamarck was right in thinking that species wer not fixed, but Cuvier was partly right about mass extinctions (p. 46).

Egyptian sculpture of an ibis

Modern ibis

Mummified ibis

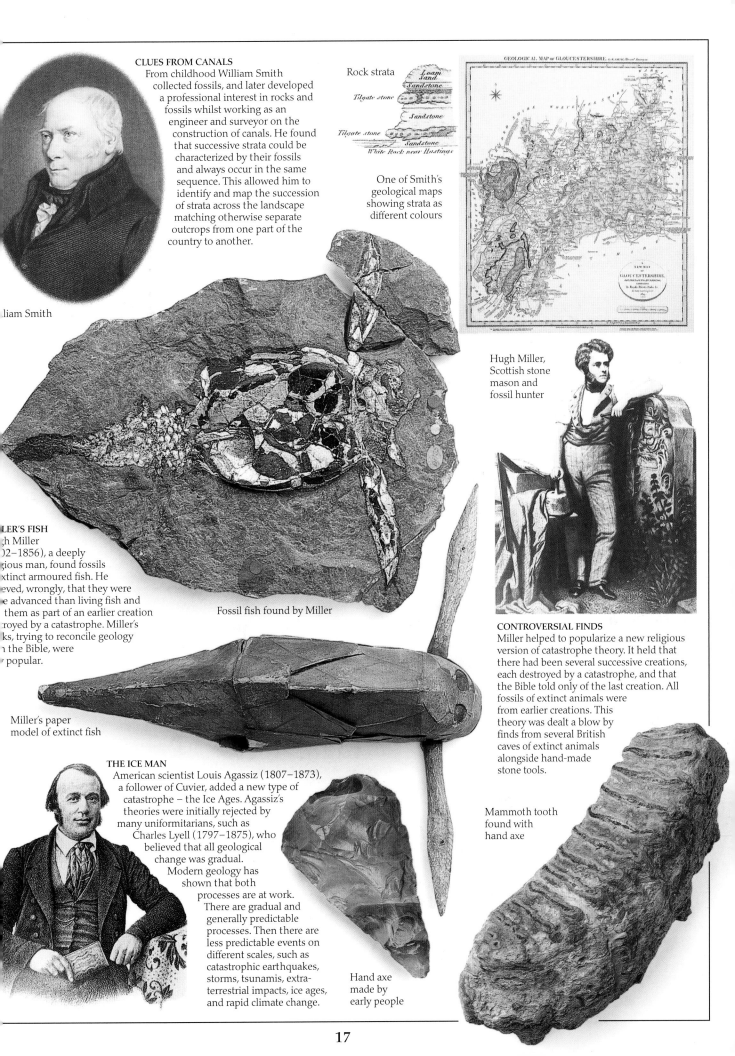

CLUES FROM CANALS

From childhood William Smith collected fossils, and later developed a professional interest in rocks and fossils whilst working as an engineer and surveyor on the construction of canals. He found that successive strata could be characterized by their fossils and always occur in the same sequence. This allowed him to identify and map the succession of strata across the landscape matching otherwise separate outcrops from one part of the country to another.

Rock strata

One of Smith's geological maps showing strata as different colours

liam Smith

Hugh Miller, Scottish stone mason and fossil hunter

LER'S FISH

h Miller
02–1856), a deeply
ious man, found fossils
xtinct armoured fish. He
eved, wrongly, that they were
e advanced than living fish and
them as part of an earlier creation
royed by a catastrophe. Miller's
ks, trying to reconcile geology
n the Bible, were
popular.

Fossil fish found by Miller

CONTROVERSIAL FINDS

Miller helped to popularize a new religious version of catastrophe theory. It held that there had been several successive creations, each destroyed by a catastrophe, and that the Bible told only of the last creation. All fossils of extinct animals were from earlier creations. This theory was dealt a blow by finds from several British caves of extinct animals alongside hand-made stone tools.

Miller's paper
model of extinct fish

THE ICE MAN

American scientist Louis Agassiz (1807–1873), a follower of Cuvier, added a new type of catastrophe – the Ice Ages. Agassiz's theories were initially rejected by many uniformitarians, such as Charles Lyell (1797–1875), who believed that all geological change was gradual.

Modern geology has shown that both processes are at work. There are gradual and generally predictable processes. Then there are less predictable events on different scales, such as catastrophic earthquakes, storms, tsunamis, extra-terrestrial impacts, ice ages, and rapid climate change.

Hand axe
made by
early people

Mammoth tooth
found with
hand axe

Dinosaur frenzy

Fossilized dinosaur bones were discovered as early as the 17th century, but they were not recognized as giant reptiles. The breakthrough came with Gideon Mantell (1804–1892), a British doctor and fossil hunter. In 1822 he found some large and unusual teeth which he showed to Cuvier (p. 16) and William Buckland, a British geologist. Both dismissed them as unimportant, but Mantell was convinced they were wrong and continued his research. Eventually he found that the teeth resembled those of iguana lizards. Calling his find *Iguanodon* (iguana-tooth), he published a description of a lizard 12 m (40 ft) long.

DIGGING FOR *IGUANODON*
Excavations at the quarry in Sussex, southern England, from which Gideon Mantell's *Iguanodon* teeth originally came.

In the meantime, Buckland had found his own giant reptile. Such finds continued, but the name dinosaur ("terrible lizard") was not used until 1841, when it was coined by Richard Owen, a celebrated anatomist and follower of Cuvier. Dinosaurs created a sensation because they were so spectacularly different from anything still alive. They remained headline news throughout the 19th century, making everyone aware of the distant past and its strange animals. This awareness set the stage for evolutionary ideas. Yet Owen used the dinosaurs as an argument against evolution, claiming that they were more advanced than living reptiles. Modern evolution theory recognizes that evolution does not always mean progress (p. 48). If the environment changes, more advanced animals can die out while their less advanced relatives survive.

SURPRISING FINDS
William Buckland (1784–1856) displays some prize specimens. The long-beaked skull at the front is an ichthyosaur, a marine reptile that belonged to a separate group from the dinosaurs. The first ichthyosaur was described in 1810 but was thought to be a crocodile. In 1824 Buckland found jaw fragments and other bones of a dinosaur called *Megalosaurus*. Richard Owen supervised the making of a model *Megalosaurus* (below) in the 1850s, before any complete dinosaur skeletons had been found. With so little evidence Owen made a good guess, but the model is largely wrong. The same sculptor made the *Iguanodon* model opposite.

CONTROVERSIAL MODELS
This model of *Megalosaurus*, based on fossils described by Buckland, was later made into a life-size dinosaur and put on show at the Crystal Palace in London alongside others. When the city fathers of New York commissioned a similar exhibition for Central Park, a local judge attacked the models as "anti-religious", and the scheme ended when someone broke into the workshop and destroyed all the models.

Jaw fragments found by Buckland

Fragments fitted into outline of skull

DARWIN'S ENEMY
Richard Owen (1804–1892), who coined the word "dinosaur", also wrote a scathing review of Darwin's *The Origin of Species* and predicted that Darwin would be forgotten in 10 years' time. In later life, Owen resented Darwin's fame and implied that he had developed an evolutionary theory of his own long before Darwin. Owen was present when, on New Year's Eve, 1853, 21 scientists ate dinner inside his model of the *Iguanodon* (below) before it joined other dinosaur models at London's Crystal Palace.

GIDEON MANTELL
On the basis of the bones and teeth that he had found, Mantell imagined *Iguanodon* to be like a large lizard. In his reconstruction Mantell placed the horn-like spike (below) on the tip of the animal's nose. It was later discovered to be a thumb spike.

Cast of *Iguanodon* "horn"

DOZENS OF DINOSAURS
In 1878 coal miners in Belgium found 39 *Iguanodon* skeletons. Fossil footprints suggested that *Iguanodon* might have walked on its hind legs. It was believed to have stood semi-upright, so the skeletons of an emu and a wallaby were studied for this Belgian reconstruction.

CHANGING IDEAS
This modern view of *Iguanodon* is based on detailed studies of marks on the bones, which can reveal much about muscles and tendons. They show that it walked mainly on two legs, with its horizontal body balanced by a rigid tail.

Misplaced thumb spike

SECRET AUTHOR
In 1844, as dinosaur discoveries amazed the public, a pro-evolution book called *The Vestiges of Creation* was published. Robert Chambers (1802–1871) was revealed as its author only after his death. Chambers aimed to make evolution respectable but was heavily criticised by scientists for inaccuracies. Even so, it was very popular and warned Darwin of potential problems.

SCALING UP
This model *Iguanodon* and other models were later scaled up to make the giant reptiles displayed at the Crystal Palace since 1854.

Charles Darwin

CHARLES DARWIN (1809–1882), THE ENGLISH NATURALIST, is well known as the author of *The Origin of Species*. He was not the first to think of evolution, and his real achievement was to present a coherent argument for evolution backed up by a mass of accurate information. In the early 19th century the concept of evolution was very unpopular. Lamarck's theory (p. 12) had been taken up in revolutionary France in the 1790s because it challenged the authority of the church and the king. The fear of a similar revolution in England made evolution a scandalous idea. Indeed, the zoologist Professor Robert Grant lost his position at the University of London and died in poverty because he openly supported Lamarck's views. When an anonymous book on evolution, *The Vestiges of Creation* (p. 19), was published in 1844, it met with outrage. All this encouraged Darwin to keep quiet for as long as possible. "It is like confessing a murder", he wrote to a friend as his theory steadily took shape in his mind. In 1858, when the naturalist Alfred Wallace also hit upon the idea of natural selection (p. 36), Darwin was finally forced to publish.

Telescope u
on the *Beag*

Charles Darwin

TAKING NOTES
While living aboard the *Beagle*, Darwin took up the habit of making careful observations of the natural world. He also made long and detailed notes, recording everything that he saw, and he thought hard about the meaning of his scientific observations.

Darwin
compas

One of Darwin's notebooks

HMS *Beagle*

From 1832 to 1836 Darwin was invited on the *Beagle*'s world voyage by Captain Fitzroy as companion and naturalist. In South America, and particularly in the Galapagos Islands, he noted many puzzling features of the plants and animals that lived there. He later understood that these peculiarities were the results of evolution.

THINKING AFLOAT
Darwin was not an evolutionist when he stepped aboard HMS *Beagle*, nor when he returned. But over the next five years the idea took shape in his mind. He was never dogmatic about his theory but considered all his opponents' views carefully. In later years this approach helped Darwin to gain support from some of the leading naturalists of his day – even those who had previously rejected evolution.

GOING ASHORE
On the voyage, Darwin took with him a copy of Charles Lyell's new book *Principles of Geology* in which Lyell claimed that the geological features of Earth could be explained by slow-acting forces that were still at work, such as the laying down of sediment. Darwin spent much time ashore, and his observations of geology confirmed Lyell's theory, implying that Earth was very old.

People of Tierra del Fuego greet the *Beagle*

A great naturalist

Before the *Beagle* voyage, Darwin studied to be a clergyman at Cambridge University. While there, he developed a passionate interest in natural history – an interest that was to change the course of his life.

Part of Darwin's beetle collection

ERASMUS DARWIN

Charles's grandfather, Erasmus Darwin (1731–1802), was a doctor, poet, and botanist. He was also a friend of scientists and industrialists, such as Joseph Priestley and Josiah Wedgwood, who questioned conventional ideas and were considered dangerous. Even before Lamarck (p. 12) he wrote a long epic poem about evolution. The next generation of the Darwin family, anxious to seem more respectable, largely ignored Erasmus's books.

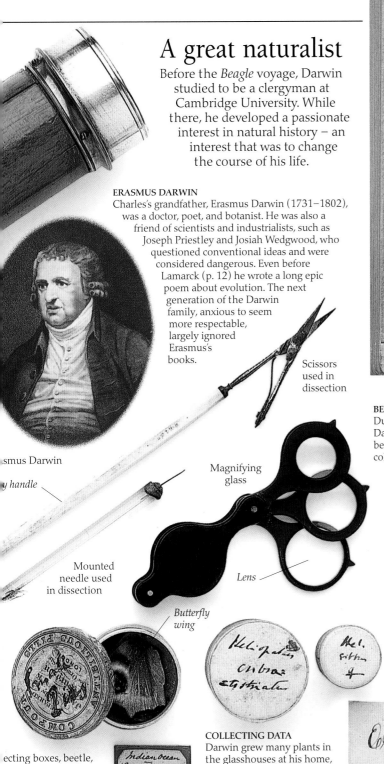

Erasmus Darwin

...y handle

Scissors used in dissection

Magnifying glass

Lens

Mounted needle used in dissection

Butterfly wing

...ecting boxes, beetle, ...microscope slide ...n Down House

BEETLE MANIA

During his student days at Cambridge, Darwin was an enthusiastic collector of beetles. This is part of his enormous collection. Being an experienced practical naturalist was a great strength for Darwin. When it came to discussing plants and animals, he had first-hand knowledge of the subject.

ALL ABOUT WORMS

After writing *The Origin of Species*, Darwin continued his work as a naturalist. He felt that looking at the small details of living things was just as important as devising grand theories. One of his later books was devoted entirely to earthworms, which clearly puzzled this cartoonist.

A cartoon from the humorous magazine *Punch*

COLLECTING DATA

Darwin grew many plants in the glasshouses at his home, Down House. He was particularly interested in climbing and twining plants, insect-eating plants, and orchids. He dissected the flowers of orchids and made some amazing discoveries about how these flowers are pollinated. Other naturalists sent him seeds or whole plants that might interest him, and some of the seed packets have survived to this day (right). Darwin's work would have made him famous as a great biologist even if he had never written *The Origin of Species*.

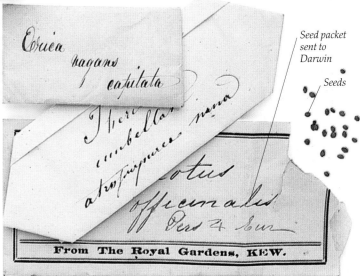

Seed packet sent to Darwin

Seeds

From The Royal Gardens, KEW.

Living evidence

DARWIN SET HIMSELF two major tasks. One was to work out a mechanism by which evolution might occur. The mechanism he thought of was natural selection (p. 36), which is still accepted today as the main force behind evolution. His other task was to collect enough evidence to convince people that evolution had occurred. Some evidence came from fossils (p. 26) or from plant and animal distribution (p. 24). Most important was the evidence from living things. This was clear enough to have been noticed by other naturalists, including Rafinesque, who wrote in 1836, "All species might have been varieties once, and many varieties are gradually becoming species". Such casual remarks by naturalists carried little weight, but Darwin was more difficult to ignore because he produced so much data. One important piece of evidence was that the same basic pattern of bones appears in the limbs of all mammals. Such similarities show that they must all be descended from a common ancestor.

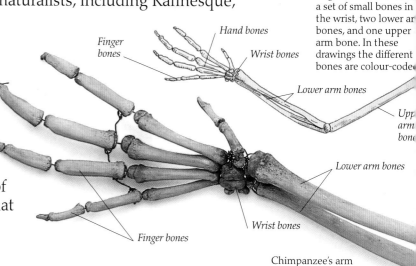

CHIMPANZEE'S ARM
The arm and hand of t[he] chimpanzee are close [to] the basic vertebrate pattern, having five fingers, five hand bone[s,] a set of small bones in the wrist, two lower ar[m] bones, and one upper arm bone. In these drawings the different bones are colour-code[d.]

Finger bones

Hand bones

Wrist bones

Lower arm bones

Upp[er] arm bone[s]

Lower arm bones

Wrist bones

Finger bones

Chimpanzee's arm

BEE ORCHIDS
These Mediterranean bee orchids look remarkably similar, but they cannot interbreed. Therefore, each of them belongs to a separate species. Each species is pollinated by a different type of insect, and this acts as an isolating mechanism (p. 41). Darwin and Rafinesque were both struck by groups of very similar species such as these. It seemed obvious that they must have evolved from a single ancestral species. This ancestor probably developed into a number of varieties or subspecies (p. 13) first.

Bat

Bones of bat's win[g]

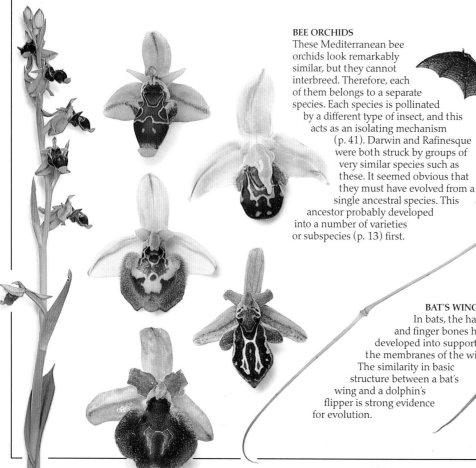

BAT'S WING
In bats, the hand and finger bones have developed into supports for the membranes of the wing. The similarity in basic structure between a bat's wing and a dolphin's flipper is strong evidence for evolution.

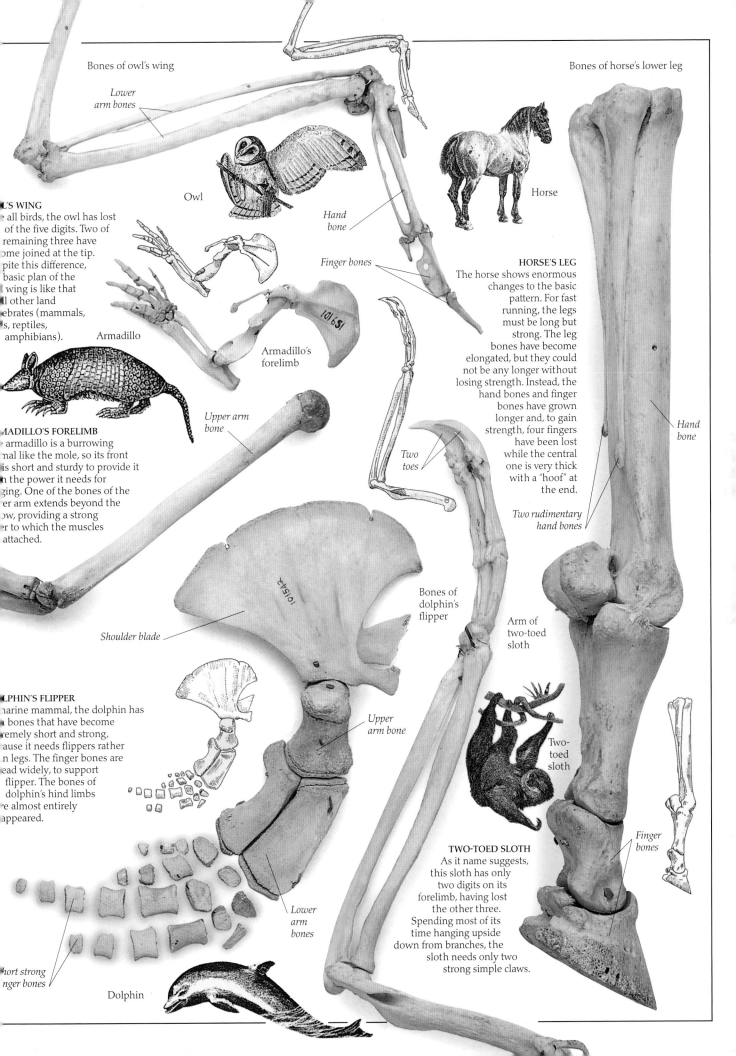

Bones of owl's wing

Lower arm bones

Owl

Hand bone

Finger bones

Bones of horse's lower leg

Horse

'S WING

all birds, the owl has lost
of the five digits. Two of
remaining three have
ome joined at the tip.
pite this difference,
basic plan of the
wing is like that
other land
ebrates (mammals,
s, reptiles,
amphibians).

Armadillo

Armadillo's forelimb

101651

HORSE'S LEG
The horse shows enormous
changes to the basic
pattern. For fast
running, the legs
must be long but
strong. The leg
bones have become
elongated, but they could
not be any longer without
losing strength. Instead, the
hand bones and finger
bones have grown
longer and, to gain
strength, four fingers
have been lost
while the central
one is very thick
with a "hoof" at
the end.

Hand bone

Two toes

Two rudimentary hand bones

ADILLO'S FORELIMB

armadillo is a burrowing
al like the mole, so its front
is short and sturdy to provide it
n the power it needs for
ging. One of the bones of the
er arm extends beyond the
ow, providing a strong
r to which the muscles
attached.

Upper arm bone

Shoulder blade

Bones of dolphin's flipper

Arm of two-toed sloth

101542

PHIN'S FLIPPER

arine mammal, the dolphin has
bones that have become
remely short and strong,
ause it needs flippers rather
n legs. The finger bones are
ead widely, to support
flipper. The bones of
dolphin's hind limbs
e almost entirely
appeared.

Upper arm bone

Lower arm bones

Two-toed sloth

Finger bones

TWO-TOED SLOTH
As it name suggests,
this sloth has only
two digits on its
forelimb, having lost
the other three.
Spending most of its
time hanging upside
down from branches, the
sloth needs only two
strong simple claws.

hort strong
nger bones

Dolphin

Animal and plant distribution

PLANT HUNTER
The botanist Joseph Hooker (1817–1911) searched for new plants in the Himalayas and New Zealand and was director of the Royal Botanic Gardens at Kew, near London. Darwin's good friend and colleague, he told him a great deal about plant distribution.

IN DARWIN'S TIME, it was believed that each species had been created by God to suit best the conditions of a particular place. This "special creation" theory had many weak points, as Darwin made clear. In Australia mammals introduced from Europe had overrun the country, wiping out some native mammals. If Australian animals were exactly right for Australia, how could this happen? Darwin showed how migration and evolution could explain the patterns of distribution far better. Islands were an important part of his argument. The animals of the Cape Verde Islands are basically like those in Africa, and the Galapagos animals are like South American animals. Since these two island groups have much the same conditions, why had the Creator not made similar animals for them? Darwin suggested that animals and plants had arrived from the nearest mainland. Some had then evolved into unique types.

Thick bony plate from the outer cover of a Glyptodon

ARMOURED ANCESTOR
While in South America, Darwin found the remains of a *Glyptodon*, a prehistoric giant armoured mammal. He realized that it resembled the living armadillos of South America. This continuity between animals of the past and present had also been found in Australia, and it provided strong supporting evidence for the idea of evolution.

Fossilized skull of *Glyptodon*

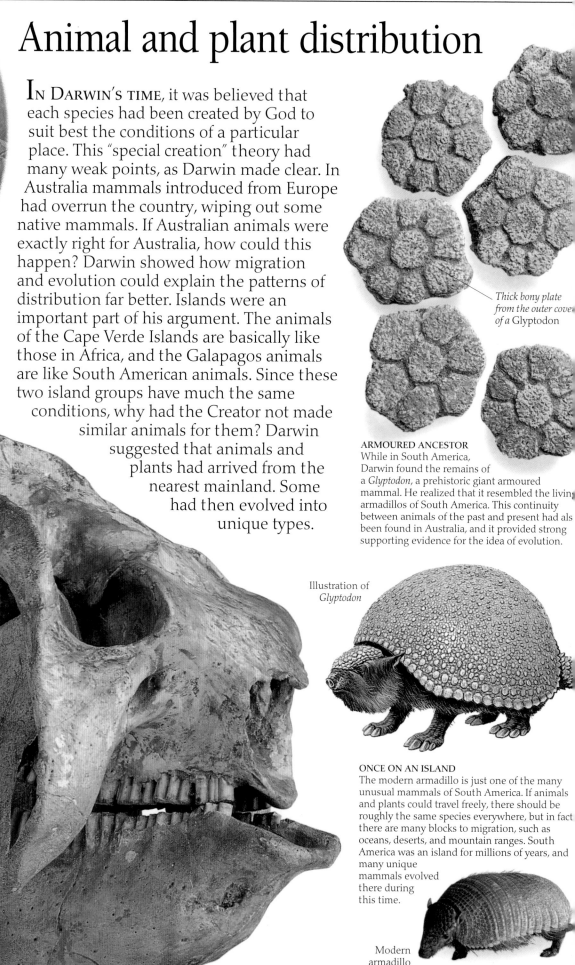

Illustration of *Glyptodon*

ONCE ON AN ISLAND
The modern armadillo is just one of the many unusual mammals of South America. If animals and plants could travel freely, there should be roughly the same species everywhere, but in fact there are many blocks to migration, such as oceans, deserts, and mountain ranges. South America was an island for millions of years, and many unique mammals evolved there during this time.

Modern armadillo

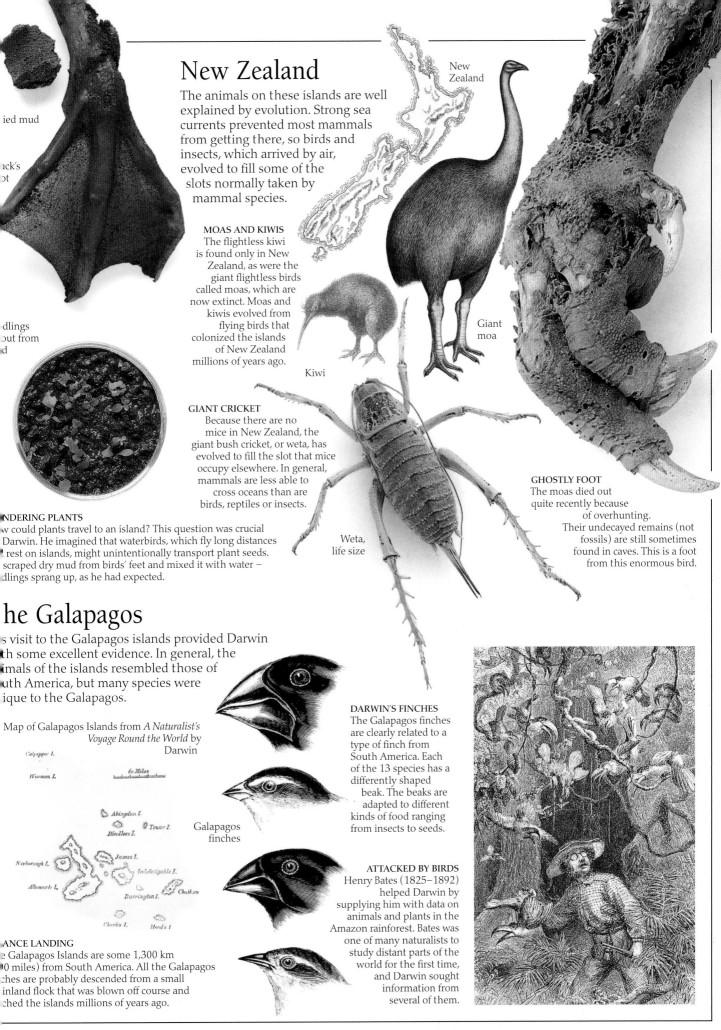

New Zealand

The animals on these islands are well explained by evolution. Strong sea currents prevented most mammals from getting there, so birds and insects, which arrived by air, evolved to fill some of the slots normally taken by mammal species.

New Zealand

MOAS AND KIWIS
The flightless kiwi is found only in New Zealand, as were the giant flightless birds called moas, which are now extinct. Moas and kiwis evolved from flying birds that colonized the islands of New Zealand millions of years ago.

Kiwi

Giant moa

GIANT CRICKET
Because there are no mice in New Zealand, the giant bush cricket, or weta, has evolved to fill the slot that mice occupy elsewhere. In general, mammals are less able to cross oceans than are birds, reptiles or insects.

Weta, life size

GHOSTLY FOOT
The moas died out quite recently because of overhunting. Their undecayed remains (not fossils) are still sometimes found in caves. This is a foot from this enormous bird.

ied mud

uck's
ot

dlings
ut from
d

NDERING PLANTS
w could plants travel to an island? This question was crucial
Darwin. He imagined that waterbirds, which fly long distances
rest on islands, might unintentionally transport plant seeds.
scraped dry mud from birds' feet and mixed it with water –
dlings sprang up, as he had expected.

he Galapagos

visit to the Galapagos islands provided Darwin
h some excellent evidence. In general, the
mals of the islands resembled those of
uth America, but many species were
ique to the Galapagos.

Map of Galapagos Islands from *A Naturalist's Voyage Round the World* by Darwin

Galapagos finches

DARWIN'S FINCHES
The Galapagos finches are clearly related to a type of finch from South America. Each of the 13 species has a differently shaped beak. The beaks are adapted to different kinds of food ranging from insects to seeds.

ATTACKED BY BIRDS
Henry Bates (1825–1892) helped Darwin by supplying him with data on animals and plants in the Amazon rainforest. Bates was one of many naturalists to study distant parts of the world for the first time, and Darwin sought information from several of them.

ANCE LANDING
e Galapagos Islands are some 1,300 km
0 miles) from South America. All the Galapagos
ches are probably descended from a small
inland flock that was blown off course and
ched the islands millions of years ago.

Fossil evidence

INSIDE STORY
Sliced in half, an ammonite reveals its intricate chambers.

Dᴀʀᴡɪɴ ꜱᴛᴜᴅɪᴇᴅ the fossil record carefully for evidence that evolution had occurred. At the time fossils did not provide him with the evidence that he needed. He hoped that fossils would bridge the evolutionary gaps between the major groups of living animals but these were not immediately forthcoming. Darwin explained their absence by arguing that the rock record was far from complete. He was also aware that many palaeontologists would use their expertise to criticize his evolutionary theory and so did not try to use fossils to support his theory. Today, we know that whilst the rock record does indeed have many gaps, there is now plenty of fossil evidence that fills the evolutionary gaps. For instance, the gradual evolution of the mammals from synapsid tetrapods is represented by a series of extinct fossils, such as the therapsid cynodonts. Darwin was also particularly concerned with the seemingly sudden appearance of life on Earth at the beginning of Cambrian times, 542 million years ago.

Hand bones

Fragments of lower arm bones

Upper a bone

Part of shoulder girdle

Ribs

Synapsid opening, seen only in mammals and mammal-like reptiles

ALMOST A MAMMAL
This is the fossilized skeleton of an animal called *Procynosuchus*, a type of extinct synapsid tetrapod (a reptile with mammalian features) known as a cynodont. It was from the cynodonts that the true mammals evolved, so they have more mammalian characters than their predecessors.

Lower jaw

Parts of shoulder girdle

Cambrian explosion

Darwin's answer to the problem of the sudden appearance of life in the Cambrian, the "Cambrian explosion", was to predict that, as more Precambrian rocks were explored, fossils would be found. This has indeed happened, and now the fossil record extends back to over 3 billion years ago, but until late Precambrian times the remains are of very primitive organisms. Even then, larger fossils, such as the soft-bodied Ediacaran fossils (p. 47), thought to be multicellular organisms, cannot yet be linked to the common early Cambrian invertebrates such as trilobites and brachiopods.

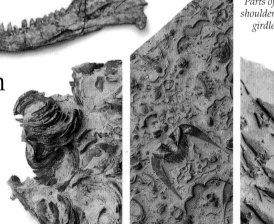

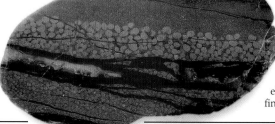

DIVERSE LIFE FORMS
These pieces of rock (left) are all from the Cambrian period, and they contain the remains of very different kinds of animals with shells – marine molluscs (far left), several kinds of trilobite, (centre), and an animal called *Ridersia*. Their appearance in the fossil record is very sudden, and their immediate ancestors remain something of a mystery.

ANCIENT CELLS
The circles on this Precambrian rock are fossil colonies of cyanobacteria, or blue-green algae. To check that these were living things, scientists can now use chemical analysis of the rock, a technique unavailab for *Eozoon* (see right). With a scanning electron microscope, even the detail of their fine structure can now be seen.

These fossil cephalopods are not a sequence of ancestors and descendants, but they give an idea of the evolutionary steps that led to the tightly coiled shells of the marine animals called ammonites (far right). The earliest stage developed a shell divided into chambers, most of which were air-filled and acted as a float. This float proved useful, but as larger species evolved, a long buoyant shell must have been hard to steer when swimming. Coiling offered a solution to this problem.

Short shell

Lengthening shell

Shell begins to coil

Shell becomes increasingly coiled and intricate

Gomphoceras

Chambered interior

Orthoceras

Phragmoceras

Cenoceras

Stephanoceras

Like a true reptile, and unlike a mammal, Procynosuchus still has ribs all along its spine, as far as the hip girdle

Lower leg bones

Upper leg bone

Pelvic (hip) girdle

HALFWAY IN BETWEEN

Many features of the skeleton of *Procynosuchus*, illustrated below, reveal its halfway position between reptiles and mammals. For example, the lower jaw is still made up of several bones, as in a reptile, while in mammals the jaw consists of just one bone. However, whereas reptiles have rows of identical teeth, *Procynosuchus* has several different types of teeth, specialized for different tasks, like a mammal. There are ribs all along the backbone as far as the hip girdle, like a true reptile, but the skull has a synapsid opening like the skull of a mammal. The legs stick out at the sides, like a lizard's, but in an emergency cynodonts could probably pull them underneath the body for more efficient running, as crocodiles can. The fossils do not tell us whether scales had evolved into fur yet, but scientists think that *Procynosuchus* may have had fur.

Part of pelvic (hip) girdle

Tail vertebrae

FALSE FOSSILS

When "fossils" were first found in Precambrian rocks in Canada, Darwin was delighted. They were given the name of Eozoon ("dawn animal"), but they turned out to be nothing more than mineral crystals.

Upper leg bone

Lower leg bones

Illustration of the complete skeleton of *Procynosuchus*

Eozoon "fossil" (19th-century drawing)

Artist's impression of *Procynosuchus*

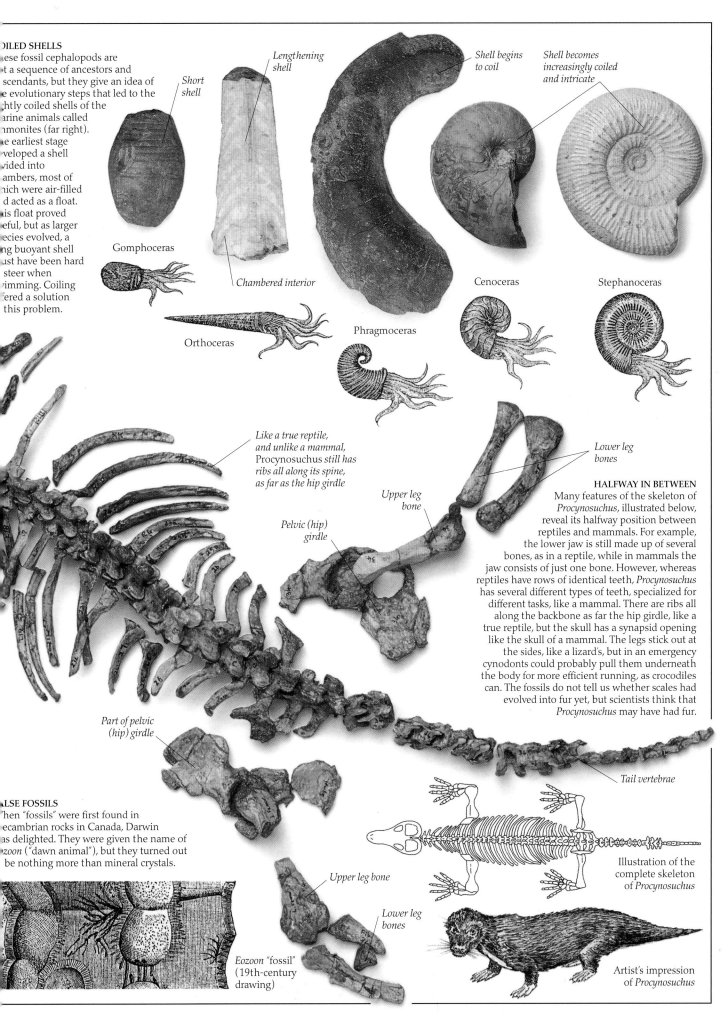

How old is Earth?

Having looked at the evidence of living things (pp. 22 and 24) and of fossils (p. 26), Darwin became convinced that evolution had occurred. At the same time, he asked himself *how* it might have occurred. In 1838 he hit on his theory of natural selection (p. 36). An obvious feature of natural selection is that it could not work quickly, because it is haphazard rather than purposeful. Darwin knew that evolution through natural selection needed an enormous amount of time, but this did not worry him, as Charles Lyell's *Principles of Geology* had convinced him that Earth was many hundreds of millions of years old. Since Lyell's time, geological research has confirmed his basic ideas, and he is known as the "father of modern geology". In 1866, however, the physicist William Thomson launched an attack on both Lyell and Darwin, claiming that Earth was, at the most, 100 million years old. Later, his figure fell to 20 million years. His calculations were based on the rate of heat loss from Earth, the present temperature of the outer crust, and the assumption that it had originally been molten. Darwin called this "one of my sorest troubles", and in later editions of *The Origin of Species* he played down natural selection, emphasizing other supposed mechanisms that he thought would work faster. Not until 1904 did Thomson's fundamental error become clear.

SLOW FORCES
The geological theories of Charles Lyell (1797–1875) were a reaction against Cuvier's catastrophe theories (p. 16). Lyell set out to explain geology using only natural forces that were still at work, rather than relying on ancient catastrophic floods as Cuvier did. Since present-day forces work very slowly, Earth must be very old, Lyell claimed.

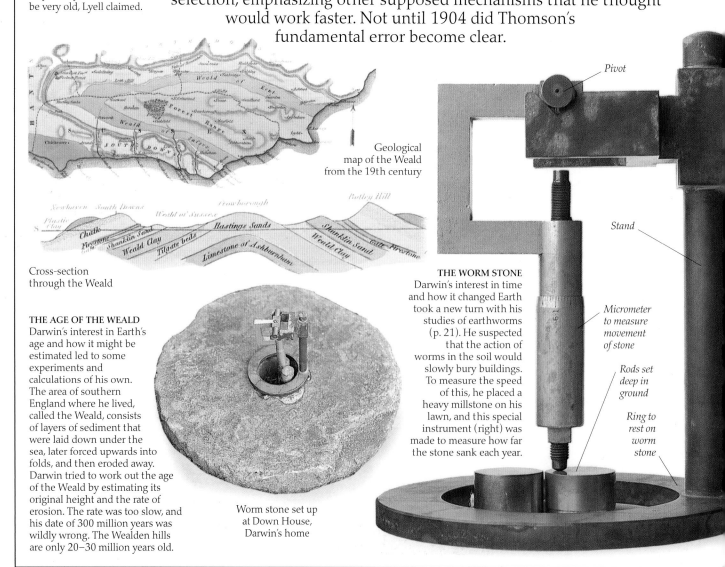

Geological map of the Weald from the 19th century

Cross-section through the Weald

THE AGE OF THE WEALD
Darwin's interest in Earth's age and how it might be estimated led to some experiments and calculations of his own. The area of southern England where he lived, called the Weald, consists of layers of sediment that were laid down under the sea, later forced upwards into folds, and then eroded away. Darwin tried to work out the age of the Weald by estimating its original height and the rate of erosion. The rate was too slow, and his date of 300 million years was wildly wrong. The Wealden hills are only 20–30 million years old.

Worm stone set up at Down House, Darwin's home

THE WORM STONE
Darwin's interest in time and how it changed Earth took a new turn with his studies of earthworms (p. 21). He suspected that the action of worms in the soil would slowly bury buildings. To measure the speed of this, he placed a heavy millstone on his lawn, and this special instrument (right) was made to measure how far the stone sank each year.

Pivot

Stand

Micrometer to measure movement of stone

Rods set deep in ground

Ring to rest on worm stone

Mica window

Early Geiger counter, used to measure radioactivity

...s-filled copper cylinder

Electrical supply

WRONG ANSWER
Radioactive emissions were discovered in 1896, and in 1903 Pierre Curie found that radium salts constantly give out heat, warming Earth's crust. Thomson was unaware of this, and it made his calculation of Earth's age entirely wrong. However, he made the arrogant claim that physics was a superior science to geology or biology. He thought that his one calculation could therefore overrule all the evidence collected by Lyell and by Darwin.

ASTRONOMER SON
George Darwin (1845–1913), one of Charles's 10 children, was a mathematician and astronomer. Asked by his father to check Thomson's calculations about the age of Earth, he concluded that they were mathematically correct. In later life, George Darwin was among the first to recognize that radioactivity was constantly warming Earth's crust, making Thomson's calculations meaningless.

LORD KELVIN
William Thomson (1824–1907) was a British physicist who later became Lord Kelvin. He and his ...llowers had some religious ...otives for attacking Darwin. Like many other people, they disliked the fact that ...atural selection showed no purpose or direction.

Insulated handle

RADIOMETRIC DATING
Radioactive elements in rocks now allow them to be dated accurately. Each radioactive element breaks down at a constant rate and always forms the same product. For example, potassium 40, found in volcanic rocks, breaks down to give argon 40. The older the rock, the more argon 40 there is. Earth's original rocks have mostly been recycled by geological processes but by measuring the age of the oldest minerals (4,400 million years) compared with the age of meteorites (4,500 million years), geologists have calculated Earth's age as 4,550 million years.

MOON ROCK
Rock samples brought back from the Moon have proved useful to geologists. The Moon and Earth were formed at the same time but, as there is no atmosphere ...n the Moon, there is no erosion. As predicted, geologists' calculations make Moon rock 4,500 million years old.

DATES CONFIRMED
Meteorites were formed at the same time as Earth. Radiometric dating shows that they are 4,500 million years old. The ages of Moon rock and meteorites have both confirmed the age of Earth that was calculated by modern geologists.

Artificial selection

IMPOSSIBLE PLANT
No one has managed yet to breed a cabbage that will grow to the size of a tree.

As **PART OF HIS SEARCH** for evidence about evolution, Darwin looked at domesticated animals and plants. During his lifetime, great progress had been made in developing new varieties of plants and animals through "artificial selection" or "selective breeding". This involves choosing those individals that have the desired qualities and breeding only from them, rejecting the rest. Knowing the extent to which certain species of plants and animals had been improved in the preceding 50 years, Darwin argued that far greater changes were possible over thousands of years. This made him suspect that all breeds of sheep, for example, were descended from a single ancestor. Other naturalists disagreed – they thought that every breed must have come from a different wild species. One naturalist even suggested that there had once been *eleven* different species of wild sheep in Britain, found nowhere else in the world. Darwin pointed out how unlikely this was, since all Britain's living mammals are also found in Europe. Subsequent evidence has shown that Darwin was correct: all the different breeds of sheep were indeed developed by selective breeding from just one ancestor. The same is true of other domesticated animals, such as cows, dogs, and horses.

ROCK DOVE
This wild bird is the raw material with which pigeon breed began. All the differ pigeon breeds kept captivity are descended from it.

DARWIN'S HOBBY
As well as his horse, Darwin kept rabbits, chickens, ducks, and pigeons. He crossed all the different breeds of pigeon and was surprised that the young often had the same colours as the rock dove, even if neither parent had them. He realized that the rock dove must be the ancestor of them all.

PIGEON BREEDS
These are some of the many different breeds of pigeon that Darwin studied. He felt that if so much change could con about through selective breeding, then similar changes could occur through the action of natural forces alone.

ANCIENT CATTLE
Wall paintings in the tombs of Ancient Egypt show cattle of many different bree Some naturalists saw such paintings as evidence that every breed was descende from a different species. After all, these breeds already existed thousands of year ago. Darwin argued that there was no reason to assume that the Egyptians wer the first farmers – selective breeding cou have begun even earlier. There is now ample evidence that his idea was correct

GIANT DOG
The Irish wolfhound is one of the largest dogs: it can be 1 m (39 in) tall at the shoulder. The smallest, the chihuahua, may stand only 20 cm (8 in) tall. Studies of their DNA (p. 52) show that all breeds of dog are descended from the European wolf.

TAIL-FREE CAT
The Manx cat has been bred to have no tail. Cats are more difficult to breed selectively than dogs, as they like to roam at night and mate as they please. Many dog breeds were developed for useful purposes, which explains why they are more varied than cats.

Manx cat

Irish wolfhound

BIG, BIGGER
Plant breeders can easily produce smaller or larger breeds, as these tomatoes show. The ancestral plant has been found in South America, and its tiny "tomato" is no larger than a redcurrant.

erry natoes

BALD DOG
The Chinese crested dog is virtually naked except for long wisps of hair on its head and tail. Breeders can alter the temperament, size, shape, and colour of a dog. Its coat can be made long or short, straight or curly.

Chinese crested dog

Giant tomato

STRANGE FRUIT
Yellow tomatoes and red grapefruit are just two of the oddly coloured fruits created by plant breeders. Darwin was convinced that artificial selection indicated a way in which evolution could occur – through a process that he called natural selection (p. 36).

SEEDLESS PRODUCE
In nature, fruits exist solely to distribute seeds. If there are no seeds inside it, a young fruit will normally wither and die. Breeders have managed to overcome this so that certain fruits, including bananas, some grapes, and some oranges, have no seeds.

Yellow tomato

Seedless orange

Pink grapefruit

All cultivated bananas are seedless

Seedless grapes

Variation and inheritance

By 1837 CHARLES DARWIN was certain that evolution had taken place, and he was thinking hard about the driving force behind it. For a while, he thought that Lamarck's theory about striving for change (p. 12) was the answer, but Darwin soon saw its weak points. He began taking an interest in anything that might answer this difficult question, including the breeding of crop plants, farm animals, and pets (p. 30). By questioning breeders, he learnt that there were small variations between individuals, which the breeders picked out. A dog breeder would choose a feature and cross two dogs carrying it. From the puppies, those that had inherited the chosen feature would be picked out and bred. If this was repeated for several generations, the feature became more and more pronounced. Darwin saw that a similar process could occur in the wild, and he called it "natural selection" (p. 36). The three ingredients needed were variation, inheritance, and competition. Inheritance clearly took place, although Darwin never really understood how. Variation between individuals was also apparent. The third factor, competition, or "the struggle for existence", was also a fact of nature (p. 34). Competition in the wild had the same role as the dog breeder, "selecting" particular individuals for breeding and discarding others.

NO TWO THE SAME
Variation is shown in the shell colours and patterns of a seashore mollusc, *Nerites*. Not all variation is as obvious as this. There may be very small variations in size or shell thickness that are not noticeable, but that affect the animal's survival. Studies of internal features show even more differences between individuals.

Varied *Nerites* shells

Norm
tea

MUTANT TEASEL
Fuller's teasel is a mutant form of the teasel plant that has curved spines on the seed-head instead of straight ones. Mutants were observed in the 19th century, but only in the 20th century were they studied systematically by geneticists (p. 51). Mutants arise through a sudden change, or mutation, in the DNA. This change occurs because the DNA is copied inaccurately when the reproductive cells are being produced (p. 53). Mutations are not dictated by the needs of the plant or animal. In fact, most mutations are damaging, and the mutants die young. But a few mutations are useful, and these are a major source of the variation on which natural selection operates.

Fuller's teasel

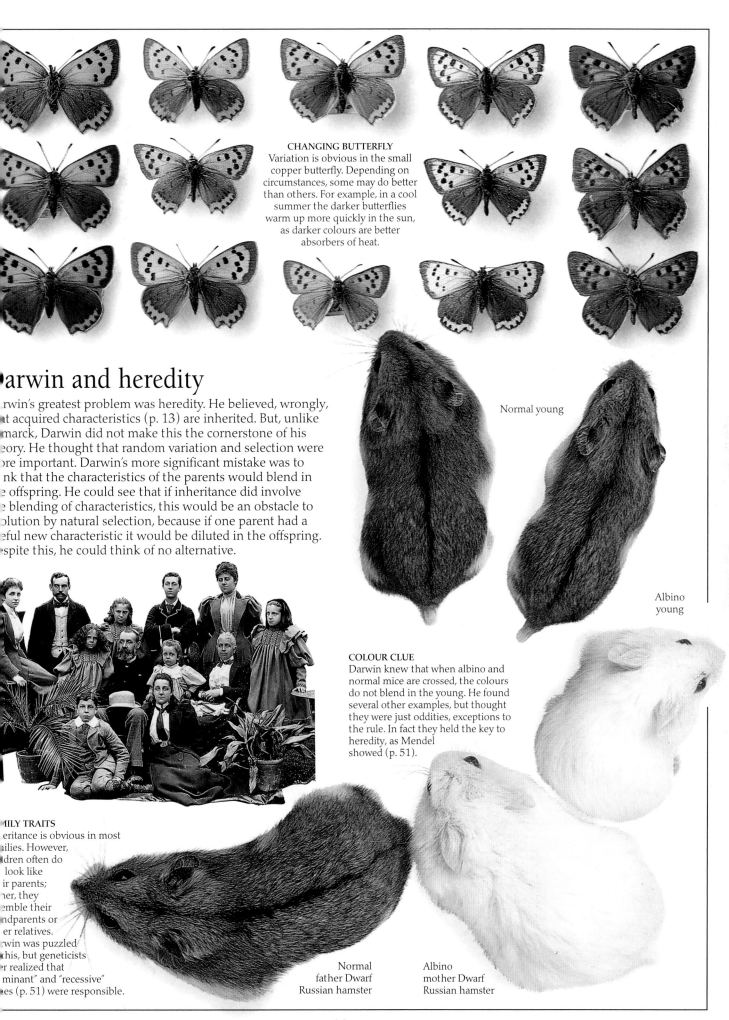

CHANGING BUTTERFLY

Variation is obvious in the small copper butterfly. Depending on circumstances, some may do better than others. For example, in a cool summer the darker butterflies warm up more quickly in the sun, as darker colours are better absorbers of heat.

arwin and heredity

rwin's greatest problem was heredity. He believed, wrongly,
t acquired characteristics (p. 13) are inherited. But, unlike
marck, Darwin did not make this the cornerstone of his
eory. He thought that random variation and selection were
re important. Darwin's more significant mistake was to
nk that the characteristics of the parents would blend in
e offspring. He could see that if inheritance did involve
e blending of characteristics, this would be an obstacle to
olution by natural selection, because if one parent had a
eful new characteristic it would be diluted in the offspring.
spite this, he could think of no alternative.

Normal young

Albino young

COLOUR CLUE
Darwin knew that when albino and
normal mice are crossed, the colours
do not blend in the young. He found
several other examples, but thought
they were just oddities, exceptions to
the rule. In fact they held the key to
heredity, as Mendel
showed (p. 51).

MILY TRAITS
eritance is obvious in most
ilies. However,
dren often do
look like
ir parents;
er, they
mble their
ndparents or
er relatives.
win was puzzled
his, but geneticists
r realized that
minant" and "recessive"
es (p. 51) were responsible.

Normal
father Dwarf
Russian hamster

Albino
mother Dwarf
Russian hamster

The struggle for existence

Many animals lay hundreds of eggs every year. Very few of these live to become adults — a fact that is obvious to any naturalist. The poet Alfred Lord Tennyson was aware of this when, in 1833, he wrote "Are God and Nature then at strife, That Nature lends such evil dreams? So careful of the type she seems, So careless of the single life". Unlike Tennyson, most people preferred to ignore the facts and see nature as happy and harmonious, a view made popular by the Reverend William Paley (p. 38). Darwin knew that plants and animals died in great numbers, but it took years for him to realize that this loss of life could be the driving force behind evolution. A naturalist and clergyman, the Reverend Thomas Malthus, helped him see the light. In 1798 Malthus had published *An Essay on the Principle of Population*, which argued that all living things tend to increase far faster than food supplies and that, in the case of humans, numbers are only kept in check by famine and disease. These ideas were well known to Darwin, but he did not actually read Malthus's essay until 1838. As soon as he read it, the idea of natural selection (p. 36) came to him in a flash, enabling him to make sense of all his earlier observations. Nevertheless, Darwin was always troubled by the "wasteful works of Nature". He consoled himself with the thought that "the war of nature is not incessant, that no fear is felt, that death is generally prompt, and that the vigorous, the healthy, and the happy survive and multiply."

STARVING THE POOR
The Reverend Thomas Malthus (1766–1834) was a kindly man, b[ut] his essay inspired a brutal new Po[or] Law in Britain. The law took welfa[re] support away from the poor unle[ss] they went into prison-like "workhouses" where husbands and wives were separated.
Feeding poor people, according to Malthus, only made poverty wors[e] in the long run, because the poor then had more children.

Dandelion flower

Tufted seeds

LUCK AND SURVIVAL
A single dandelion flower produces dozens of seeds. The wind blows them away, and there is no guarantee that they will land on soil where they can flourish. Most never grow into plants. Chance clearly plays the major part in deciding which seeds arrive in a good spot. But for those that survive this stage, new struggles begin: struggles for moisture, light, and space. In these contests, chance plays less of a part, and the plant's own qualities become more important.

Dandelion "clock" with dry seeds ready to disperse

Dandelion head after the seeds have been blown away

Dozens of seeds from a single head

HUNTER AND PREY
A thin and hungry polar bear pursues a nimble arctic fox across the snow. One of the most important parts of the struggle for survival is the need to eat – and the need to avoid being eaten by others.

̣GHTING FOR SPACE
̣ke most seabirds, gannets are vulnerable to predators ̣hen nesting, so they nest only on small, rocky islands ̣ere there are no rats or foxes to destroy their eggs ̣d young. As suitable islands are few, they become ̣y crowded. Competition between animals for nesting ̣es is another aspect of the "struggle for existence".

̣roglets set
̣ff into the
̣ide world

̣ggs

Frog's spawn

RED IN TOOTH AND CLAW
The poet Alfred Lord Tennyson wrote his poem *In Memoriam* in 1833, 25 years before Darwin published *The Origin of Species*. It includes the memorable line "Nature red in tooth and claw". This phrase later came to symbolize people's hatred for the idea of natural selection. They reacted as if Darwin had invented the struggle for existence, rather than simply described it.

THE NUMBERS GAME
A frog can lay hundreds of eggs in a single year. If all these survived to adulthood and produced young of their own, the world would be knee-deep in frogs within 10 years. Clearly, most of them die. Some of the eggs and tadpoles are killed by fungi, some by predators. Others die from lack of food. Of the few dozen froglets that may survive each year, only one or two are likely to live long enough to breed.

Adult frog

Natural selection

HOW DOES EVOLUTION OCCUR? Charles Darwin's answer was through "natural selection". He realized that there was always some variation between individuals within a species (p. 32), so that some are a little larger, some have thicker fur, or slightly longer legs. He also realized that there is a struggle for existence (p. 34) because more individuals are born than can survive. To some extent, chance plays a part in deciding which ones survive, but the characteristics of the individual must sometimes make a difference. The animal with longer legs will run faster and thus escape a predator. The animal with thicker fur will survive a cold winter. Only those that survive have the chance to produce young ones – and that is where inheritance (p. 33) is important. If the slightly longer legs or thicker fur are passed on to some of the offspring, then more animals have those useful characteristics in the next generation. After hundreds of generations, these small changes may add up to a large and noticeable difference. Darwin proposed that this process produces adaptation (p. 38) and could also produce new species, given enough time (p. 40). The idea of natural selection came to Darwin in 1838, but he spent a further 20 years working on the idea and collecting more evidence. He was nervous about the controversies that his theory might provoke, and this too made him delay publication. Had Alfred Wallace (above left) not reached similar conclusions, Darwin might never have published at all.

GREAT MINDS
In 1858 British naturalist Alfred Wallace (1823–1913) wrote to Darwin from Malaya, asking advice on a short article he had written. To Darwin's dismay it contained the idea of natural selection. Wallace did not know that Darwin had been working on this idea for 20 years. A joint publication was hastily arranged.

WINTER KILLS
Killed by the cold and lack of food, this eagle has lost forever its chance of producing young. Another eagle, with thicker feathers, or better hunting abilities, may survive to produce chicks next spring.

Moths on light bark

Industrial pollution in 19th-century England

Moths on dark bark

CONCEALING COLOURS
In the 19th century a good example of natural selection occurred in the industrial regions of northern England, although no one grasped its significance at the time. The peppered moth rests on tree trunks by day. Its pale dappled wings are camouflaged against lichens growing on the trunks, and this protects the moth from insect-eating birds. Pollution kills off lichens, and as industry grew, the tree trunks turned black with soot from factory smokestacks. Dark versions of the peppered moth arose by mutation (p. 32) and were better camouflaged than the original form. Gradually, the dark forms became more and more common.

Sexual selection

Apart from natural selection, Darwin also identified another important mechanism: sexual selection. When animals mate, they are choosy about their partners. Usually it is the female choosing the male, or males fighting to control females. Sometimes, however, females must compete for males, or both partners may be choosy. The qualities that ensure success differ widely, from physical strength to bright feathers. Only those chosen as mates pass on their characteristics to the next generation.

Single tail feather from male peacock

Flowers

Well-fed plant with plentiful flowers that will produce more seeds and thus more offspring

FIGHTING FOR MATES
Male elephant seals fight for the right to breed. On the beaches where they come to breed every year, only a few males gain a territory. These territory-holders, the ones who can fight off their rivals, herd together a "harem" of females and mate with all of them. This type of sexual selection produces great size and strength in the males. The female seals are less than half their size.

Vigorous growth

How does it begin?

It is easy to see how natural selection can make fur thicker or legs longer, but how does a totally new feature develop? In every case, there must be something for natural selection to work on, an existing feature that can be modified to make the new one.

Meat being placed on leaf

PPEALING TAIL
exual selection often volves males tracting females. eacocks display their ils to females, who oose the best-looking ale. Bright feathers ay originally have en favoured because ey showed that a ale was healthy, it once this process gins, the feathers ay become more d more elaborate.

Few flowers

Unfed plant

HUNGRY PLANTS
The leaves of the sundew plant have evolved to become insect traps. Most plant leaves can absorb some nutrients directly, and this must have been the starting point for the ancestor of sundews. They grew in bogs with poor soil, and small insects that happened to drown on their damp leaves would have supplied extra minerals. Natural selection would then have favoured plants that increased this nutrient supply. If a plant with stickier leaves appeared, it would do better than others, because small flies would become stuck on the leaves. Darwin experimented with sundews, feeding some with small pieces of meat and keeping others unfed. Those fed on meat grew more quickly, produced more flowers, and set more seeds. He had shown that being able to trap and digest insects would be a characteristic favoured by natural selection.

Understanding adaptation

Moles have strong, broad front feet for digging through soil. Ducks have webbed feet for swimming. Polar bears have very thick fur. It is clear to any naturalist that all plants and animals are superbly adapted to their climate and way of life. Darwin proposed that these adaptations were an outcome of natural selection. However, there was already a powerful and popular theory about adaptation known as "natural theology". This interpreted all adaptation as evidence of the creator's handiwork. *Natural Theology, or Evidences of the Existence and Attributes of the Deity*, by the English clergyman William Paley, set out the ideas most fully. Published in 1802, Paley's book was widely read. While studying for the clergy as a young man, Darwin had read and admired it, not thinking that he would one day be its greatest critic. Fortunately, the two opposing theories can each be tested against the facts. Natural theology predicts that all adaptations should be perfect. Evolution through natural selection predicts that they should be influenced by (and often limited by) the past.

William Paley
(1743–1805)

PALEY'S WATCH
William Paley began *Natural Theology* with an example to prove his basic point. He imagined himself walking across a heath and finding a watch among the stones. Unlike the stones, the watch has moving parts that work together for a purpose. The existence of the watch would prove that there was a watchmaker. Paley drew a parallel between a watch and an animal. Just as the watch proved the existence of a watchmaker, so an animal (or a plant) proved the existence of a Creator. By studying natural history, the nature of God could be better understood.

What purpose?
Inspired by natural theology, naturalists set out to find God's intended "purpose" for each living thing, a difficult task, especially in the case of pests such as rats and fleas. In Darwin's view, the only "purpose" of any creature is a private one – to survive and produce young. If it does this, it has succeeded in passing on its characteristics to the next generation.

ECHOES OF CREATION?
Bats navigate by making high-pitched sounds and listening for the echoes. Some have elaborate nose-leaves to channel the sound. Can such devices be produced by natural selection, or must there be a "watchmaker", a creator? The fact is that there are many simple versions of this "radar" among bats, and a range of intermediate forms leading up to the most complex ones. This has convinced biologists that such features can, and have, evolved.

Faces of leaf-nosed bats

European mole

Long, thin hand and finger bones support wing

SAME BONES
The bat's spreading wing and the mole's stubby digging arm have the same set of bones, as do the arms of all mammals (p. 23). This astonishing similarity only makes sense if Darwin was correct and they come from the same distant ancestor.

Strong arm for digging

Leaf-nosed bat

ar from perfect

cording to Natural Theology, the adaptations
iving things should be perfect. According to
rwin, adaptations are always restricted
the ancestry of the plant or animal,
cause natural selection can only work
the raw material available. If the raw
terial is not ideal for the purpose, or natural
ection has not had long enough to work,
adaptations will be less-than-perfect.

Panda's
paw

rs occasionally attack
er animals

THE PANDA'S THUMB

Bears are mostly omnivores, and their paws have
five very short "fingers". Giant pandas, descended
from bears, eat bamboo shoots and need a thumb
to hold them. In fact, they have evolved one,
but it is a short, imperfect thumb jutting
out from the wrist. It seems that the
bear's paw was too specialized for natural
selection to "reverse" the basic plan
and make a true thumb. Instead, the
panda's false thumb has grown from
a bone in the wrist.

*False
thumb*

STILL ADAPTING

Many people suffer
from backache, or
problems with their hips,
knees, or feet, while pain in
the arms is rare. In Darwin's
terms, this makes sense.
Humans are unusual among
mammals in standing
upright. The fossil evidence
suggests that we only
began to do so between
5 and 8 million years ago.
The human back and legs
have not yet had time
to adapt fully.

ate
d

Giant panda

Human
spine

GATE BIRD PUZZLE

win pointed out that
h frigate birds and
and geese have
bed feet, yet neither
s into the water.
explained their
as a leftover from
ir past, both
ng descended
m waterbirds.
hey were
igned by a
ator, Darwin
ndered, why
they have
se useless
tures?

DESIGN FAULT

Loons, or divers, can scarcely walk on land
(below), because their legs are set so far back on
the body. Most diving birds have the legs set
well back, because this is the best position for
efficient swimming. The penguin (left) has solved
the problem of walking by adopting an upright
stance. For the loon, upright walking may evolve in
time. A "watchmaker" might have made the loon more
mobile on land by standing it upright, or by adding
another pair of legs near the middle.

King penguin

Red-throated
diver

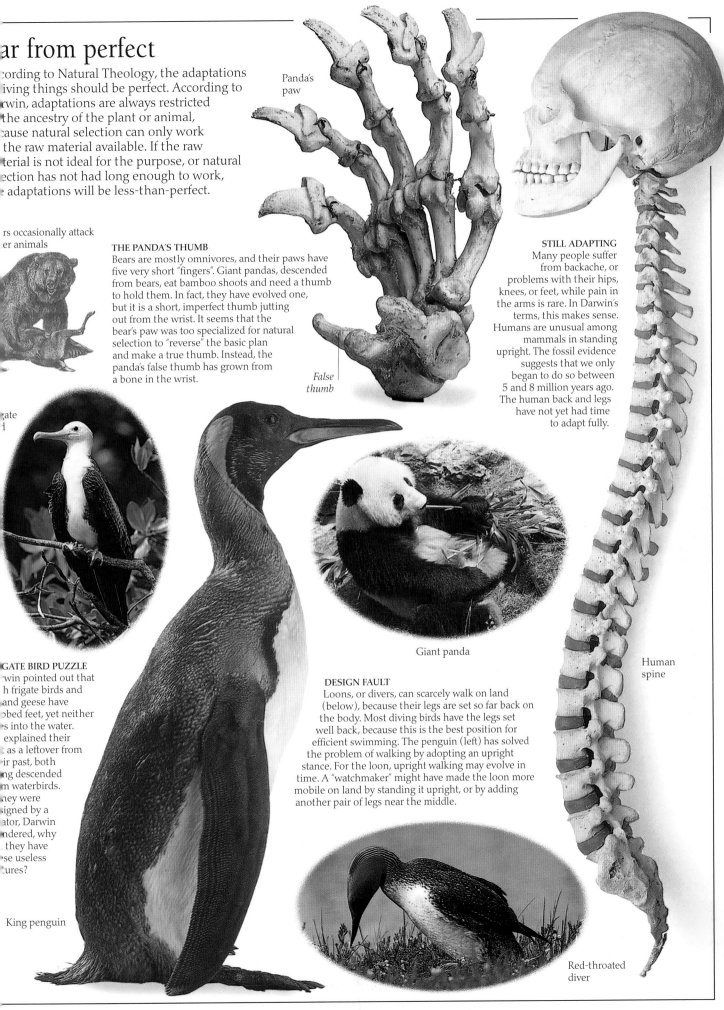

How new species are formed

ALTHOUGH DARWIN called his book *The Origin of Species*, he said very little about how new species might arise. In fact, he called this the "mystery of mysteries". Today the process is better understood, although there are still disagreements about the details. In general, most new species arise when a population becomes cut off from the rest of its kind, especially if it then lives in conditions that differ from those of the parent species. This might happen, for example, when birds are blown off course and reach distant islands (p. 25) or cross a mountain range. Sheer distance can also be a physical barrier, as in the case of a ring species (below). Under new conditions, or simply because they are isolated, the population may begin to evolve in a different direction and may develop into a new race or subspecies. In time, that subspecies can change so much and become so different from the rest of its species that the two can no longer interbreed. Once this happens, they are two distinct species. Occasionally, a new species may arise in other ways, without any geographical isolation.

THE COMTE DE BUFFON
Georges Buffon (1707–1788) of France was the first to define a species as a group of living things that can all potentially interbreed with each other, but not with members of other species.

Herring gull
(*Larus argentatus argentatus*)

Lesser black-backed gull (*Larus fuscus graellsi*)

ONE SPECIES OR TWO?
The herring gull (left) and the lesser black-backed gull (right) are descended from gulls that lived in eastern Siberia. These ancestral gulls spread out to both east and west. In time, the two lines of migration met on the other side of the globe, over northern Europe. The two ends of this circle are the herring gull and the lesser black-backed gull. These birds have changed so much from their common ancestor that they do not interbreed, except very rarely.

RING SPECIES
Each of the different subspecies of herring gull interbreeds with its neighbours, as do the different subspecies of lesser black-backed gull. In eastern Siberia, the herring gulls interbreed with neighbours that are called black-backed gulls, but could just as well be called herring gulls. These gulls form a "ring species" and show how new species can arise through accumulated small changes.

Larus argentatus vegae

Larus argentatus birulaii

Larus fuscus antellus

Larus fuscus heuglini

Larus argentatus omissus

Larus fuscus fuscus

North Pole

Larus argentatus smithsonianus

Larus argentatus argentatus

Larus fuscus graellsi

Isolating mechanisms

A new species may develop in isolation, but often it moves back into the area where the "parent" species lives. The two species may still be similar enough to mate and produce young, although these hybrid offspring are infertile (unable to have young themselves). For the parents, producing such a hybrid is a waste of time and energy, so it pays them to recognize their own species. They do so using signals such as smell, sound, colour, or behaviour. These signals, which keep species apart, are called "isolating mechanisms".

Chiff-chaff   Wood warbler   Willow warbler

NOT ONE, BUT THREE

The English naturalist Gilbert White (1720–1793) was the first to notice that the chiff-chaff, the willow warbler, and the wood warbler were three different species, not just one. The wood warbler is slightly larger and brighter in colour, but the chiff-chaff and willow warbler look almost exactly the same. The songs of these three, however, are distinctly different. For the birds, songs are used by the female to select a mate, so in this way they act as an isolating mechanism, separating the otherwise similar species.

CHOOSING A MATE

Butterflies, which fly by day, recognize potential mates by their patterns and colours. Moths, which fly by night, rely more on scent. For many species, there are also internal mechanisms that prevent fertilization between different species. These are especially important in plants.

South American Sweet Oil butterflies mating

GETTING IT RIGHT

These butterflies have made the right choice of mate, but this is not always the case. Mistakes are occasionally made because isolating mechanisms, like adaptations (p. 39), are a product of evolutionary change and are not necessarily perfect. For example, a horse may mate with a donkey, producing a mule, which is infertile.

Asian swallowtails mating

PERFUMED PARTNERS

Mice and many other mammals recognize their own species by characteristic scents. In some species, specific courtship rituals are performed. These are used to confirm that the correct choice of partner has been made.

KEPT APART

Theodosius Dobzhansky (1900–1975) worked with T.H. Morgan on fruit flies (p. 51) and helped in the synthesis of genetics and evolutionary theory. He coined the term "isolating mechanisms" for the biological barriers that discourage crossing between different species.

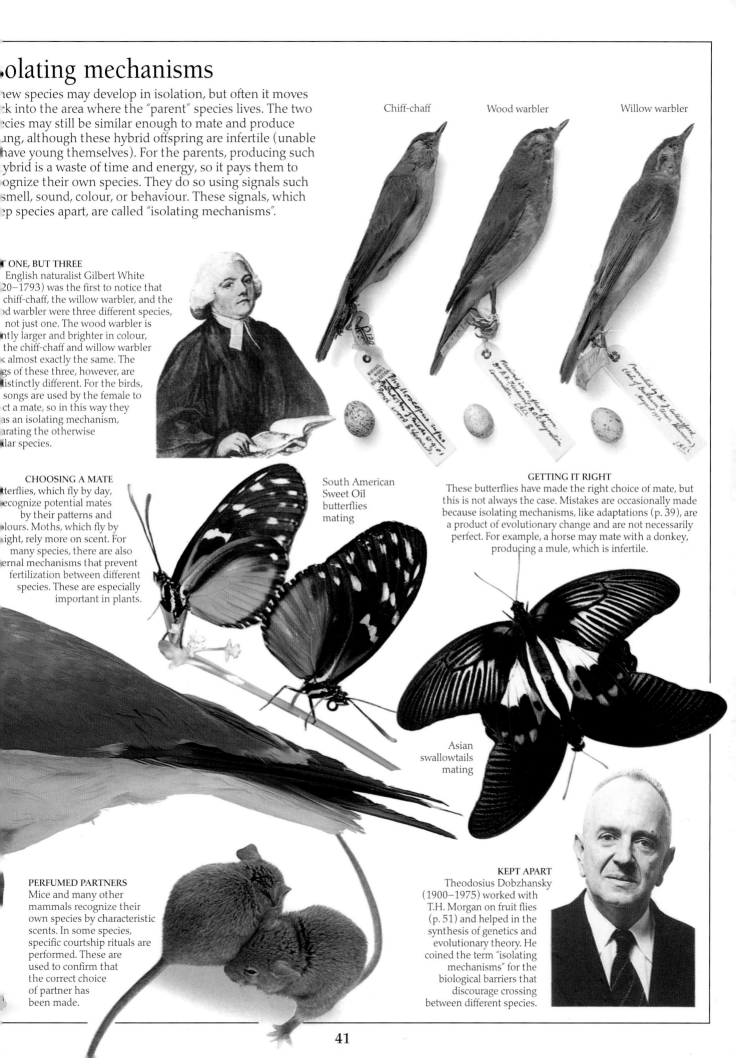

Living intermediates

GRADUAL GLIDING
Flying squirrels do not really fly, but glide from tree to tree. Gliding animals could have gradually evolved from ordinary tree-dwellers by acquiring flaps of skin that broke their fall when jumping. Some gliders could then have evolved into flying animals such as birds and bats.

DARWIN BELIEVED THAT natural selection could produce adaptations (p. 38), but could it produce animals with a completely different way of life? Could it turn a marine animal into a land animal, or a non-flier into a flier? How might such major alterations be achieved through a series of small changes? Some transitional fossils have been found that help to answer this question (p. 44), and "living intermediates" help to make sense of the fossils. These living forms, such as lungfish and egg-laying mammals, are not the ancestors of other animals living today, but they may be related to those ancestors or may have followed a similar evolutionary path. In the case of lungfish, comparisons with fossils show that many extinct lungfish and other air-breathing fish flourished 380 million years ago. The climate was hot and dry, so pools and streams may have been shrinking and stagnant. Lungs must have evolved to allow fish to gulp air at the surface. Fossils show that the evolution of the basic four-limbed (tetrapod) structure developed within a group of fish with paired muscular fins, like those of the Australian lungfish, whilst they were still mostly aquatic in habit. Thus these fish were pre-adapted with tetrapod limbs before they used them for life on land. As for any major transition, the move from life in the water onto land required the acquisition of more than one character, namely lungs to breathe air and limbs for movement on land. A similar bit-by-bit transition is seen in birds. New discoveries of feathered and winged but still land-living dinosaurs show how the transition to early birds, such as *Archaeopteryx* (p. 45), and evolution of flight probably occurred.

ASA GRAY (1810–1888)
American evolutionist Asa Gray also considered the problem of intermediates. Darwin wrote to him, "The eye to this day gives me a cold shudder, but when I think of the known fine gradations, my reason tells me I ought to conquer the cold shudder". Objectors to evolution claimed that the human eye could not have evolved by steps, but living intermediates show that it could.

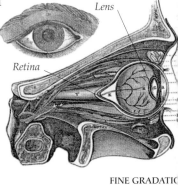

Lens

Retina

FINE GRADATIC
The simplest eyes are just clumps of lig sensitive cells. Found in snails, they car no more than distinguish light from de In higher animals, a transparent lens evolved to focus light on to th light-sensitive cells, wh now form the ret

AUSTRALIAN LUNGFISH (be
Lungfish, of which there are r only six species, can gulp air at surface, allowing them to liv stagnant water containing l oxygen. Lungfish and other breathing fish flourished million years ago when stagn pools were probably a comr feature of the landsc

FLYING FISH
Darwin observed that flying fish "now glide far through the air, slightly rising and turning by the aid of their fluttering fins". If they had evolved into true fliers, Darwin asked, who would then have imagined that "in an early transitional state they had used their incipient organs of flight [fins] exclusively to escape being devoured by other fish?"

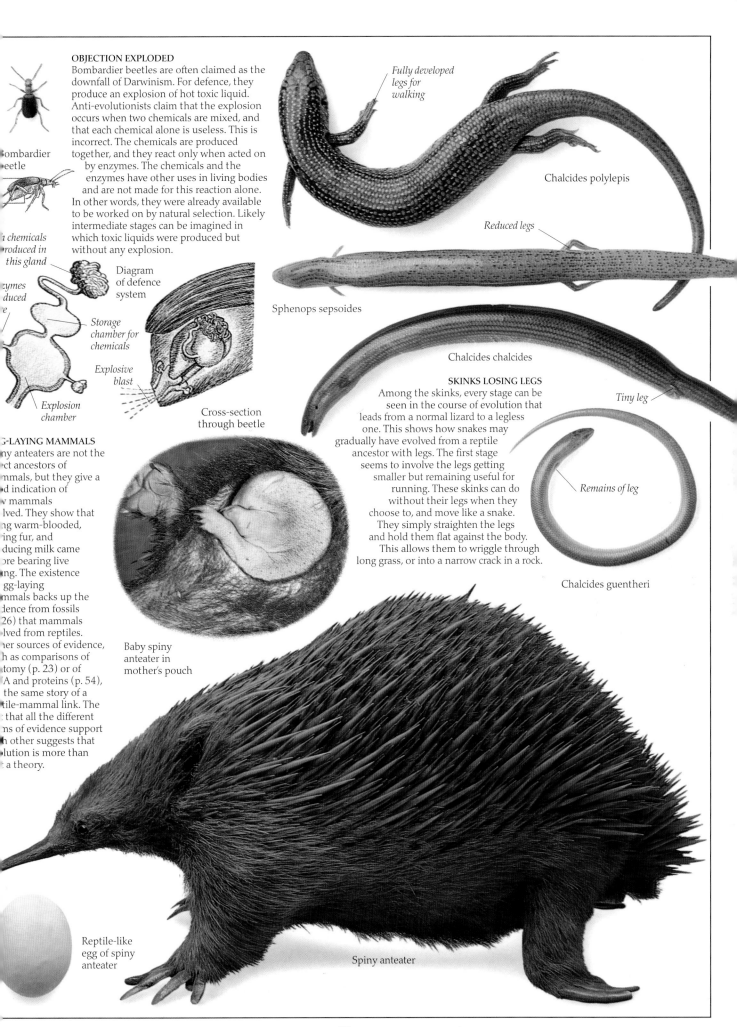

OBJECTION EXPLODED

Bombardier beetles are often claimed as the downfall of Darwinism. For defence, they produce an explosion of hot toxic liquid. Anti-evolutionists claim that the explosion occurs when two chemicals are mixed, and that each chemical alone is useless. This is incorrect. The chemicals are produced together, and they react only when acted on by enzymes. The chemicals and the enzymes have other uses in living bodies and are not made for this reaction alone. In other words, they were already available to be worked on by natural selection. Likely intermediate stages can be imagined in which toxic liquids were produced but without any explosion.

ombardier
eetle

chemicals
roduced in
this gland

zymes
duced

Diagram
of defence
system

Storage
chamber for
chemicals

Explosive
blast

Explosion
chamber

Cross-section
through beetle

Fully developed
legs for
walking

Chalcides polylepis

Reduced legs

Sphenops sepsoides

Chalcides chalcides

SKINKS LOSING LEGS

Among the skinks, every stage can be seen in the course of evolution that leads from a normal lizard to a legless one. This shows how snakes may gradually have evolved from a reptile ancestor with legs. The first stage seems to involve the legs getting smaller but remaining useful for running. These skinks can do without their legs when they choose to, and move like a snake. They simply straighten the legs and hold them flat against the body. This allows them to wriggle through long grass, or into a narrow crack in a rock.

Tiny leg

Remains of leg

Chalcides guentheri

G-LAYING MAMMALS

ny anteaters are not the
ct ancestors of
mmals, but they give a
d indication of
v mammals
lved. They show that
ng warm-blooded,
ing fur, and
ducing milk came
re bearing live
ng. The existence
gg-laying
mmals backs up the
ence from fossils
26) that mammals
lved from reptiles.
er sources of evidence,
as comparisons of
tomy (p. 23) or of
A and proteins (p. 54),
the same story of a
tile-mammal link. The
that all the different
ns of evidence support
other suggests that
lution is more than
a theory.

Baby spiny
anteater in
mother's pouch

Reptile-like
egg of spiny
anteater

Spiny anteater

43

Fossil intermediates

LIKE LIVING INTERMEDIATES (p. 42), fossil intermediates can reveal how new groups evolved from existing ones. They are not a perfect guide, however, because the full set of intermediates is very rarely found. It has been estimated that only one fossil species is found for every 20,000 species that have lived, so the chances of finding an actual ancestor of a living group is very small. The most that scientists can hope for is to find a fossil species that was related to such an ancestor. This means that some guesswork must be used in reconstructing past events. However, the guesses made are based on a great deal of careful study of the fossils, and of living things. All ideas about how things evolved are repeatedly tested and questioned by other scientists. When new fossils are found, they are used to test existing theories about the past and may confirm or disprove those theories. Among the fossils that have helped to reveal the course of evolution are those of early frogs (below). Fossil frogs show that broad skulls came before features such as very long legs. Broad skulls and mouths are typical of animals that catch fast-moving prey underwater, so it seems that this led the way in frog evolution.

ANCIENT ELEPHANT
Together with other fossils, the 35-million-year-old fossil *Phiomia* (pictured in this artist's impression) shows how elephants, mammoths, and mastodons evolved from relatively small, hippo-like animals.

Artist's impression of *Mi...* from 50 mill... years ...

HALFWAY THERE
Fossil skeletons of *Miacis* show th... it was on the evolutionary line leading to martens and stoats. Fos... of *Miacis* have been found in coal seams, the remains of ancient den... forests, in Germany.

Artist's impressio... 20-million-y... old *Enaliar...*

ANCIENT SEA DOG
Another fossil, *Enaliarctos*, reveals how dog-like ancestors evolved in... sea lions. It probably fed in the sea, but spent more time on land than living sea lions.

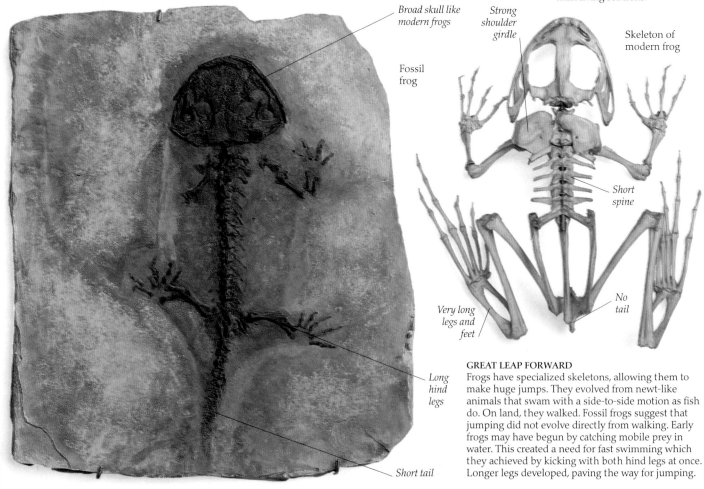

Broad skull like modern frogs

Fossil frog

Strong shoulder girdle

Skeleton of modern frog

Short spine

Very long legs and feet

No tail

Long hind legs

Short tail

GREAT LEAP FORWARD
Frogs have specialized skeletons, allowing them to make huge jumps. They evolved from newt-like animals that swam with a side-to-side motion as fish do. On land, they walked. Fossil frogs suggest that jumping did not evolve directly from walking. Early frogs may have begun by catching mobile prey in water. This created a need for fast swimming which they achieved by kicking with both hind legs at once. Longer legs developed, paving the way for jumping.

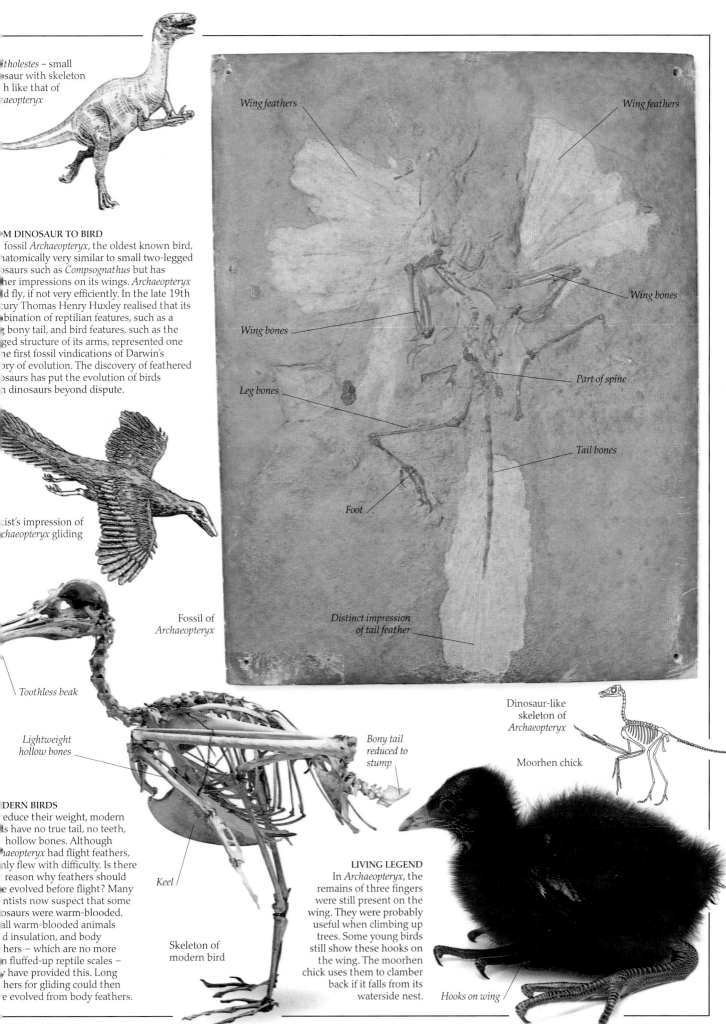

*...tholestes – small
...saur with skeleton
...h like that of
...aeopteryx*

...M DINOSAUR TO BIRD
... fossil *Archaeopteryx*, the oldest known bird,
...natomically very similar to small two-legged
...osaurs such as *Compsognathus* but has
...her impressions on its wings. *Archaeopteryx*
...ld fly, if not very efficiently. In the late 19th
...tury Thomas Henry Huxley realised that its
...bination of reptilian features, such as a
..., bony tail, and bird features, such as the
...ged structure of its arms, represented one
...he first fossil vindications of Darwin's
...ory of evolution. The discovery of feathered
...osaurs has put the evolution of birds
...n dinosaurs beyond dispute.

*...ist's impression of
...chaeopteryx gliding*

Toothless beak

*Lightweight
hollow bones*

...DERN BIRDS
...educe their weight, modern
...ls have no true tail, no teeth,
... hollow bones. Although
...haeopteryx had flight feathers,
...nly flew with difficulty. Is there
... reason why feathers should
...e evolved before flight? Many
...ntists now suspect that some
...osaurs were warm-blooded.
...ll warm-blooded animals
...d insulation, and body
...hers – which are no more
...n fluffed-up reptile scales –
...y have provided this. Long
...hers for gliding could then
...e evolved from body feathers.

Keel

Skeleton of
modern bird

Wing feathers

Wing feathers

Wing bones

Wing bones

Part of spine

Leg bones

Tail bones

Foot

Fossil of
Archaeopteryx

*Distinct impression
of tail feather*

Dinosaur-like
skeleton of
Archaeopteryx

Moorhen chick

*Bony tail
reduced to
stump*

LIVING LEGEND
In *Archaeopteryx*, the
remains of three fingers
were still present on the
wing. They were probably
useful when climbing up
trees. Some young birds
still show these hooks on
the wing. The moorhen
chick uses them to clamber
back if it falls from its
waterside nest.

Hooks on wing

Jumps and gaps

WHILE THERE ARE MANY INTERMEDIATE forms found in the fossil record (pp. 26 and 44), there are also many jumps and gaps. Evolutionists can now explain some of these, but not all. The most puzzling is the sudden appearance of many new and fairly complex animals in the Cambrian period (p. 26). This is still not fully understood, but scientists continue to investigate the issue. A second puzzle, the dramatic changes in fossils at the end of the Palaeozoic era and the Mesozoic era, are now fairly well explained (below). A third problem is the lack of intermediates that bridge the gap between many groups, especially invertebrates. It seems that intermediate forms are relatively rare, perhaps because changes occur rapidly, and only in one small area of the world. This would mean that few intermediates become fossils. As a comparison, if a multi-storey car park was "fossilized" by a fall of volcanic ash, there would be plenty of cars fossilized on each level, but the chances of a car being fossilized while driving up from one level to the next would be relatively small.

THE CAMBRIAN EXPLOSION
This fossil arthropod from the Burgess shale in the Canadian Rocky Mountains belongs to the Cambrian period at the start of the Palaeozoic era (below), when many new animals suddenly appeared. No definite ancestors have yet been identified.

CHANGING ERAS
As the early geologists noted (p. 16), the fossils from one geological period differ from those of another. The differences between the three major eras (Precambrian, Palaeozoic, and Mesozoic) which each include several geological periods (p. 60), are even greater, as these three pieces of fossil-bearing rock show. The major differences between the fossils from successive eras are due to mass extinctions.

END OF THE MESOZOIC
The Arizona meteorite crater is a recent example of the many impact events that have affected Earth and its life. The Mesozoic Era ended 65 million years ago with a major extinction event, coinciding with a giant 11-km (7-mile) wide meteorite crashing into the Gulf of Mexico. Life was devastated and groups such as the ammonites and dinosaurs died out, except for the small, feathered dinosaurs we know as birds.

Rock containing fossilized sea shells and remains of trilobites

2 MESOZOIC
Triassic rock, containing ammonites, belongs to the Mesozoic era, the age of dinosaurs. Both dinosaurs and ammonites became extinct at the end of this era, 65 million years ago, when some 60 per cent of species died out.

1 PALAEOZOIC
This piece of rock is from the Silurian period in the Palaeozoic era. This era ended 251 million years ago, when more than 90 per cent of species became extinct. The cause is unknown, but a dramatic change in the condition of the atmosphere and oceans is the likely cause.

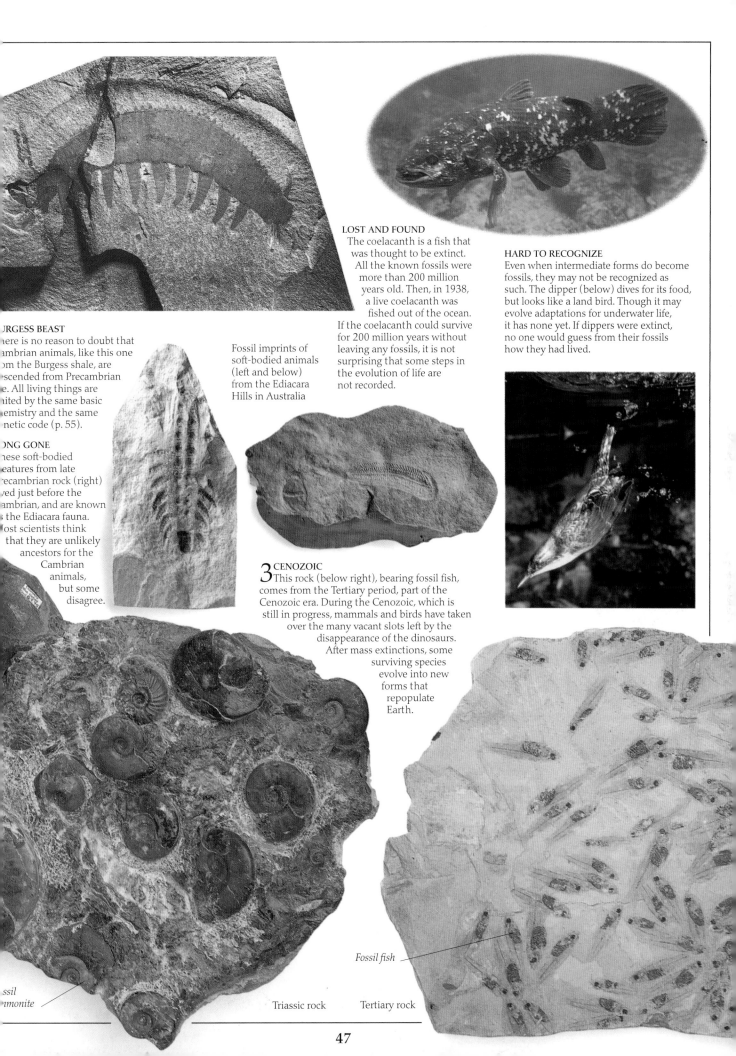

LOST AND FOUND

The coelacanth is a fish that was thought to be extinct. All the known fossils were more than 200 million years old. Then, in 1938, a live coelacanth was fished out of the ocean. If the coelacanth could survive for 200 million years without leaving any fossils, it is not surprising that some steps in the evolution of life are not recorded.

HARD TO RECOGNIZE

Even when intermediate forms do become fossils, they may not be recognized as such. The dipper (below) dives for its food, but looks like a land bird. Though it may evolve adaptations for underwater life, it has none yet. If dippers were extinct, no one would guess from their fossils how they had lived.

[B]URGESS BEAST

[T]here is no reason to doubt that [C]ambrian animals, like this one [fr]om the Burgess shale, are [de]scended from Precambrian [lif]e. All living things are [un]ited by the same basic [ch]emistry and the same [ge]netic code (p. 55).

[LO]NG GONE

[Th]ese soft-bodied [cr]eatures from late [P]recambrian rock (right) [liv]ed just before the [C]ambrian, and are known [as] the Ediacara fauna. [M]ost scientists think that they are unlikely ancestors for the Cambrian animals, but some disagree.

Fossil imprints of soft-bodied animals (left and below) from the Ediacara Hills in Australia

3 CENOZOIC

This rock (below right), bearing fossil fish, comes from the Tertiary period, part of the Cenozoic era. During the Cenozoic, which is still in progress, mammals and birds have taken over the many vacant slots left by the disappearance of the dinosaurs. After mass extinctions, some surviving species evolve into new forms that repopulate Earth.

Fossil fish

[Fo]ssil
[am]monite

Triassic rock   Tertiary rock

Ladders and branches

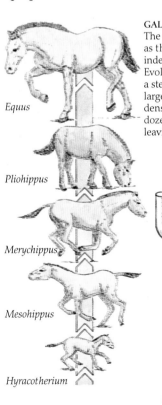

ALL FOR PROGRESS
Ernst Haeckel (1834–1919) developed the idea of "evolution as progress" to its fullest extent. He believed that nature had been deliberately moving towards a final goal: human beings. The more that is discovered about what happened in the past, the less this idea makes sense.

In 19TH-CENTURY Europe and North America the "Industrial Revolution" was changing everyone's lives. Towns were growing rapidly, a network of railways was spreading, and new factories were drawing thousands of workers from the countryside to the cities. Almost every aspect of social life was in a process of change. Most people, especially those in power, believed that all these changes amounted to "Progress", and that progress must be good. Evolution was a controversial idea for religious reasons, and linking it to progress made it far more acceptable. Darwin himself refrained from making this connection because he knew that the reality of evolution did not quite fit in with such ideas. For example, many types of bacteria have stayed small and simple for billions of years without "progressing" to become larger or more complex. This is also true of many other living things whose evolutionary history is more like a branching bush of diversification than a ladder of constant improvement. However, Darwin did not try to contradict two of his followers, Thomas Huxley and Ernst Haeckel, both of whom presented evolution in terms of progress. This rapidly became the popular view, and the idea is still widespread today.

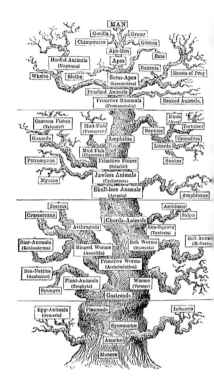

ECHOES OF THE PAST
As well as putting humans at the top, Haeckel's tree contains another of his theories: recapitulation. He believed that as an embryo developed it went through all the evolutionary stages of its ancestors. The five "ancestors" at the bottom of the tree trunk are based on the very early stages of development of an embryo.

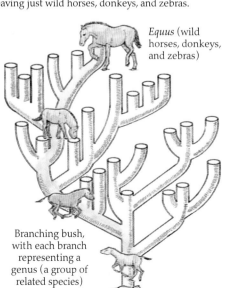

GALLOPING UP
The evolution of the horse is often shown by a diagram such as this (left). Although the fossils of all these ancestors have indeed been found, this "ladder" gives a false picture. Evolution does not go in straight lines, and it is not always a steady march of progress from small-and-simple to large-and-complicated. A more realistic image is a densely branching bush (below). There have been dozens of species, most of which have died out, leaving just wild horses, donkeys, and zebras.

Equus

Pliohippus

Merychippus

Mesohippus

Hyracotherium

Equus (wild horses, donkeys, and zebras)

Branching bush, with each branch representing a genus (a group of related species)

"DARWIN'S BULLDOG"
Thomas H. Huxley (1825–1895) was a young, energetic English scientist who took up the cause of evolution in many public debates. He fought on behalf of Darwin, who preferred to keep out of the public eye. However, Huxley was inspired by Haeckel, and he distorted Darwin's ideas with notions of "progress".

OUR MISSING TAIL (*below*)
The mistaken idea of recapitulation contains a grain of truth. Young embryos do resemble the embryos of related animals. For example, at about four weeks of age the human embryo (below) has a set of parallel grooves like those that lead to gill slits in fish. It also has a tail at this stage, which is later lost. The embryo does develop in a way which sometimes echoes its evolutionary past, but it does not re-enact every step of its evolution as Haeckel suggested.

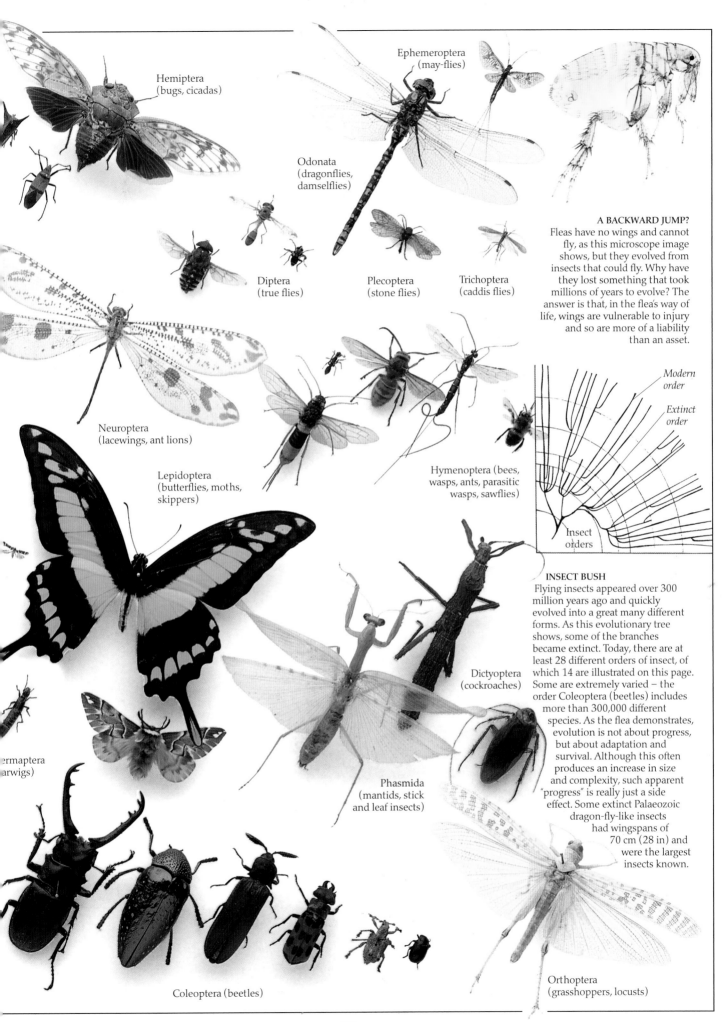

Hemiptera
(bugs, cicadas)

Ephemeroptera
(may-flies)

Odonata
(dragonflies,
damselflies)

Diptera
(true flies)

Plecoptera
(stone flies)

Trichoptera
(caddis flies)

A BACKWARD JUMP?
Fleas have no wings and cannot
fly, as this microscope image
shows, but they evolved from
insects that could fly. Why have
they lost something that took
millions of years to evolve? The
answer is that, in the flea's way of
life, wings are vulnerable to injury
and so are more of a liability
than an asset.

Neuroptera
(lacewings, ant lions)

*Modern
order*

*Extinct
order*

Hymenoptera (bees,
wasps, ants, parasitic
wasps, sawflies)

Insect
orders

Lepidoptera
(butterflies, moths,
skippers)

INSECT BUSH
Flying insects appeared over 300
million years ago and quickly
evolved into a great many different
forms. As this evolutionary tree
shows, some of the branches
became extinct. Today, there are at
least 28 different orders of insect, of
which 14 are illustrated on this page.
Some are extremely varied – the
order Coleoptera (beetles) includes
more than 300,000 different
species. As the flea demonstrates,
evolution is not about progress,
but about adaptation and
survival. Although this often
produces an increase in size
and complexity, such apparent
"progress" is really just a side
effect. Some extinct Palaeozoic
dragon-fly-like insects
had wingspans of
70 cm (28 in) and
were the largest
insects known.

Dictyoptera
(cockroaches)

...rmaptera
...rwigs)

Phasmida
(mantids, stick
and leaf insects)

Coleoptera (beetles)

Orthoptera
(grasshoppers, locusts)

Gregor Mendel

GREGOR MENDEL
The talented and intelligent son of poor peasants, Mendel could continue his science studies only by entering the local monastery. Many of his fellow monks were enthusiastic scientists.

GREGOR MENDEL (1822–1884) was a monk and a physicist. Some of his fellow monks were crop breeders, and he began investigating heredity to help them to improve their crops. Being a physicist, he looked for simple laws that could be expressed mathematically, and this happened to be a good way of approaching heredity. By an inspired guess, Mendel chose to study "either/or" characteristics, such as seed colour in peas. Others scientists were looking at characteristics that appear to blend in the offspring, such as size. Though these are more common, they are far more difficult to study. Mendel's results, published in 1865, were not understood until 1900, when scientists made the same discoveries again. "Mendelism" was born, and in 1909 the word "gene" was coined for his hereditary particles (p. 52). At first Mendelism seemed to oppose Darwinism, because "either/or" characteristics would not create the small variations on which natural selection could work. In the 1920s it was realized that most characteristics are governed by dozens of genes, each with small effects that can add up to a large effect. The many genes controlling a characteristic such as size can provide small variations, but each gene behaves in exactly the same way as a gene for an "either/or" characteristic. The ideas of Mendelism clearly supported Darwin, and they were combined in a new theory – neo-Darwinism.

Variety 1 Self-fertilizing — yy Alleles in plants — yy Alleles in seeds

Variety 2 Self-fertilizing — YY Alleles in plants — YY Alleles in seeds

Seeds

Variety 1 pollinated by variety 2 — Cross-pollination — Variety 2 pollinated by variety 1

Allele in egg — Y Y — Alleles in pollen — Yy Yy Yy Yy — Alleles in seeds

Y Y — Allele in egg — Yy Yy Yy Yy — Alleles in seeds

Hybrid plant self-fertilizes (any hybrid seed from either plant will give the same result)

Yy Alleles in plant

Y or y Allele in egg
Y or y Allele in pollen
YY Yy Yy yy Alleles in seeds

MINIATURE TREES
Bonsai trees, like trees grown in harsh natural conditions, show how much external forces influence a characteristic such as size. The tree's genes (its "genotype") provide the raw material, but what happens to the tree helps to shape its actual form (the "phenotype"). To study heredity, it is important to look at characteristics that are not affected by external factors, or to keep the external factors exactly the same.

Tree stunted by severe pruning

Bonsai yew, less than 30 cm (1 ft) ta

A branch of normal yew, a tree that grows to a height of 25 m (82 ft)

inding genes

...ndel worked with plant ...ieties (different types ...hin a species). He crossed ...ieties that had distinct, ...ntrasting characteristics, ...ch as seed colour. His ...ults showed that heredity ...s not blending, but ...olved discrete units, ...w called genes.

...OSSING PEAS (*left*)
...ndel crossed a green-seeded ...iety of pea with a yellow one. ...a flowers normally fertilize ...mselves, but they can be fertilized ...hand with pollen from another ...nt.) All the seeds from the cross ...re yellow. These seeds were ...nted, and the plants were allowed ...self-fertilize. They produced ...low and green peas, in a ratio of ... This ratio reveals what is ...pening inside the plants. As ...ndel realized, there must be ...editary particles (now called ...es) that do not divide or blend. In ...s case, there is a single gene for ...d colour, but two different ...sions (or alleles) of the gene. One ...le codes for yellow, the other for ...en. Each seed carries two alleles, ...d if they are of different types then ... seed is yellow: the allele for ...low (called the dominant) masks ... effect of the allele for green ...led the recessive). Each seed ...eives one allele from the pollen ...d one allele from the egg.

...I MORGAN (1866–1945)
...omas Hunt Morgan began work ...fruit flies in 1907. By 1911 he had ...own that genes were located on the ...romosomes. His work helped lead to ... realization that most characteristics ...controlled by many genes.

Red ink

Blue ink

Red and blue inks mixed to produce purple

Red beads

Blue beads

Red and blue beads mixed to produce purple; each bead represents a single allele of one gene for flower colour

BLENDING QUALITIES
If a plant variety with red flowers is crossed with another variety having blue flowers, the offspring usually have purple flowers. It appears that the effect is like that of mixing inks.

Inks cannot be separated

SEPARATING PARTICLES (*below*)
Heredity actually depends on particles called genes, but for most characteristics dozens of genes are involved, not just one as for the colour of peas. Each gene has a small effect, but together they can add up to a large effect. The mixture of red and blue beads shows how the combined action of many genes can give a result that resembles blending inheritance, but this result is only superficial. By breeding from the purple-flowered hybrids, it is possible to get blue plants and red plants again. Like beads, the genes can be separated out again.

Unlike inks, different coloured beads can be separated out again

BRED IN BOTTLES
Fruit flies (*Drosophila*) are far easier to study than plants. They can be kept in bottles, they breed quickly, and they often undergo spontaneous changes (called mutations) in their genes. Through his work on these flies, Morgan managed to locate each gene at a specific site, or "locus", on a chromosome. Chromosomes are situated in the nucleus, at the centre of every cell.

Tiny mutant fruit fly

Normal fly

This "White Miniature Forked" has three mutations

Normal fly

SEEING GENES
Fruit flies offer an added bonus to geneticists – they have giant chromosomes in their salivary glands, and because of their size these can be studied more easily than normal chromosomes. Each band on the chromosomes corresponds to an individual gene site, or "locus". Genes are now known to consist of DNA (p. 52).

Solving the DNA puzzle

BY THE 1920S, it was clear that the chromosomes (p. 51) carry the genes. Chromosomes were found to contain both deoxyribonucleic acid (DNA) and protein, and no one knew which was the hereditary material. James Watson (b. 1928) and Francis Crick (1916–2004) guessed that it was DNA; they hoped that, by working out its structure, they could understand heredity. They had seen X-ray images of DNA, and they knew the shape and chemistry of its various components. Using all this information, they tried to work out the structure by building models. Success came in 1953 and, as they had hoped, the structure revealed how heredity worked. The molecule is like a ladder twisted into a double helix. The rungs of the ladder are made up of chemical compounds called bases, two per rung (called a base pair). There are four different types of base (adenine, cytosine, thymine, and guanine). The breakthrough for Watson and Crick was the realization that adenine could pair only with thymine, and guanine could pair only with cytosine. They saw that this would enable DNA to divide and yet produce perfect copies of itself, and that the order of the bases along the molecule could contain the genetic information.

X-RAY VISION
Rosalind Franklin (1921–1958) studied crystals of DNA using X-ray diffraction. The way in which the crystals scatter the X-rays reveals the structure and chemistry of the molecules in the crystal. Rosalind Franklin's images confirmed earlier theories about DNA, that its molecule is indeed a double helix.

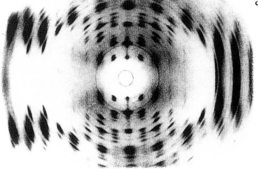

MAPPING MOLECULES
Rosalind Franklin's X-ray diffraction pictures also revealed that the sugar and phosphate units of DNA were on the outside of the helix. This was vital information for Watson and Crick.

Base p

Base pair

Strand he

Strand of helix

DOUBLE HELIX
This illustration show the different base pai that make up the rungs of the DNA molecule. Each base will only fit with one other base.

STRANDS OF LIFE
In order to copy itself, the DNA molecule divides. The two strands of the helix come apart, little by little, as the base pairs separate. Then new bases pair on to the existing ones on each strand. The fact that each base can only pair with one other base ensures that each half of the original helix becomes an exact copy of the complete original. This is how the hereditary information is passed on from one generation to the next. Occasionally, however, a mistake can occur in the copying, and this results in a genetic mutation (p. 32). Mutations can provide a valuable source of raw material for evolution.

Orig DNA mole

Base

Copies forming

WINNING MODEL (*left*)
This is part of the original model of the DNA molecule, made by James Watson (left) and Francis Crick (right) in 1953. The base pairs, or rungs, are arranged along the strands of the DNA molecule in what seems like a random order. In fact, the order of the bases is full of information and can be translated according to the "genetic code".

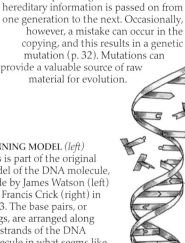

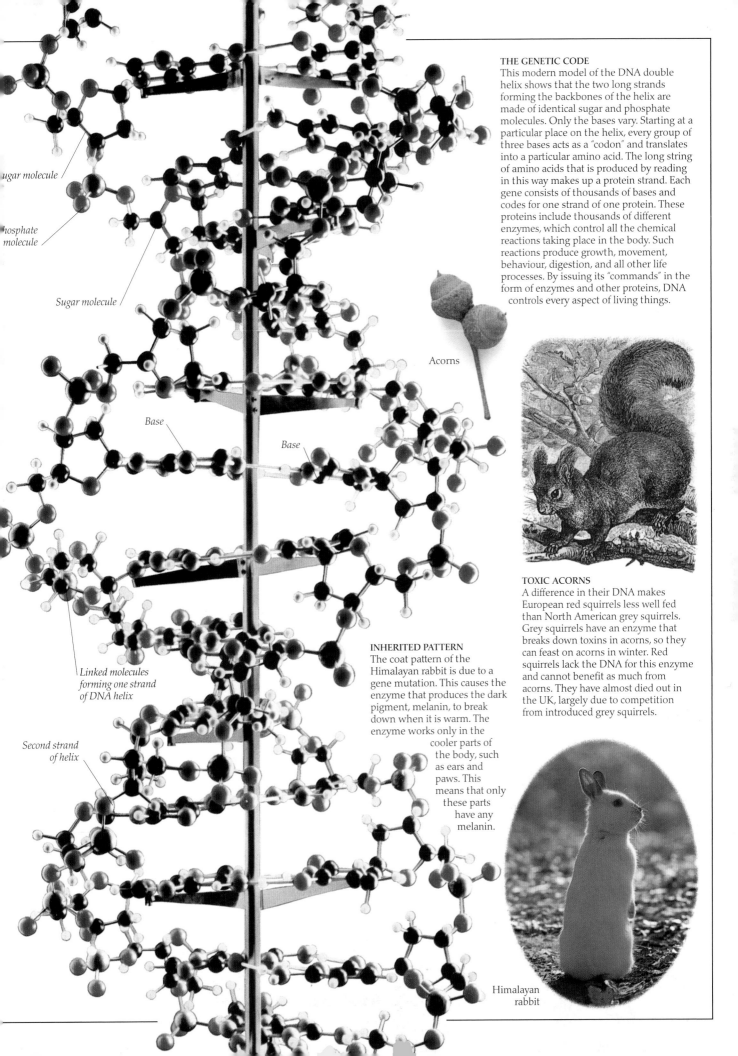

ugar molecule

hosphate
molecule

Sugar molecule

Base

Base

Linked molecules
forming one strand
of DNA helix

Second strand
of helix

Acorns

THE GENETIC CODE
This modern model of the DNA double
helix shows that the two long strands
forming the backbones of the helix are
made of identical sugar and phosphate
molecules. Only the bases vary. Starting at a
particular place on the helix, every group of
three bases acts as a "codon" and translates
into a particular amino acid. The long string
of amino acids that is produced by reading
in this way makes up a protein strand. Each
gene consists of thousands of bases and
codes for one strand of one protein. These
proteins include thousands of different
enzymes, which control all the chemical
reactions taking place in the body. Such
reactions produce growth, movement,
behaviour, digestion, and all other life
processes. By issuing its "commands" in the
form of enzymes and other proteins, DNA
controls every aspect of living things.

TOXIC ACORNS
A difference in their DNA makes
European red squirrels less well fed
than North American grey squirrels.
Grey squirrels have an enzyme that
breaks down toxins in acorns, so they
can feast on acorns in winter. Red
squirrels lack the DNA for this enzyme
and cannot benefit as much from
acorns. They have almost died out in
the UK, largely due to competition
from introduced grey squirrels.

INHERITED PATTERN
The coat pattern of the
Himalayan rabbit is due to a
gene mutation. This causes the
enzyme that produces the dark
pigment, melanin, to break
down when it is warm. The
enzyme works only in the
cooler parts of
the body, such
as ears and
paws. This
means that only
these parts
have any
melanin.

Himalayan
rabbit

Molecular evidence

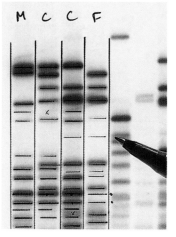

DNA FINGERPRINTS
Comparing DNA is a useful way of finding out how closely living things are related. Here DNA from two children (C and C) is being compared with DNA from each of their parents (M and F). This version of the method is called "DNA fingerprinting". It can be used to identify the father of a child, for example. DNA fingerprints can also be taken from blood stains, and these are sometimes used to help in the identification of criminals.

Sɪɴᴄᴇ ᴛʜᴇ ᴡᴏʀᴋ ᴏꜰ Watson and Crick (p. 52), scientists have continue to study DNA. They have found that DNA itself, and the proteins it produces, contain vital evidence about evolution. If two new species evolve from a common ancestor, their DNA, and thus their protein molecules, slowly begin to change and build up differences. The number of differences is proportional to the time since they separated. This discovery was made in the 1960s and a possible explanation was proposed by a Japanese scientist, Motoo Kimura. He suggested that ma mutations (p. 32) have neither good nor bad effects. He called these "neutral mutations". Such a mutation could change one of the amino aci in a protein molecule (p. 53) without affecting how the protein does its job in the body. Kimura's theory is still disputed, but the fact that mutations build up at a regular rate is not in doubt. It is as if the molecu inside the body carry a steadily ticking clock that creates a record of the past. This can be used to check the accuracy of evolutionary trees worke out from fossils or from comparisons of the structure of living things. This independent source of evidence largely confirms the evolutionary trees already worked out, indicating that scientific ideas about evolution are correct.

DEEP FROZEN
The bodies of now-extinct mammoths a sometimes found in the icy ground of Siberia. These remains still contain DNA although it is partially broken down. Thi ancient DNA can be compared with tha the mammoth's relative, the elephant.

Family tree of elephants and their close relatives

- African elephant
- Asian elephant
- Mammoth (extinct)
- Mastodon (extinct)
- Steller's sea cow (extinct)
- Dugong
- West Indian manatee
- Brazilian manatee
- West African manatee
- Hyrax
- Aardvark
- Other mammals

60   40   20   0
Time scale (millions of years ago)

PROTEINS FROM THE PAST
One simple way of comparing proteins is to use the immune system. This is the system that animals have for defence against disease. It reacts to foreign substances very specifically, so if an animal such as a rabbit has been "vaccinated" with proteins from an elephant, its immune system will also react to proteins from a relative of the elephant, for instance a mammoth, but not as strongly. The closer the relationship, the stronger the reaction. The family tree (left) for elephants and their close relatives was worked out in this way.

Preserved mammoth from Siberia

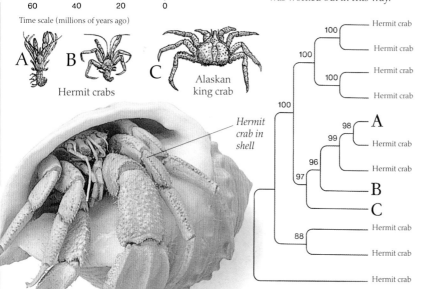

A   B   C   Alaskan king crab

Hermit crabs

Hermit crab in shell

- 100 — Hermit crab
- Hermit crab
- 100 — Hermit crab
- 100 — Hermit crab
- 100
- 98 — A
- 99 — Hermit crab
- 96
- 97 — B
- C
- Hermit crab
- 88 — Hermit crab
- Hermit crab
- Hermit crab

TESTING A THEORY
Hermit crabs are small and depend on the shells of molluscs for their homes. Because of their habit of living in spiral shells, the hind-part of the body, the abdomen, is curved to one side. Alaskan king crabs are large and never live in mollusc shells, but zoologists suspected that they had evolved from hermit crabs because their abdomens are slightly assymmetrical, like those of hermit crabs. When DNA comparisons became possible, zoologists saw a way of testing this theory. They extracted DNA from many different species of hermit crab and from Alaskan king crabs. Comparisons showed that king crabs are indeed very closely related to the hermit crabs (left). As with the mammoths, elephants, and sea cow, the DNA confirmed what was already thought on the basis of more traditional evidence.

E

F

G

Insect

Flowering
plant

SAY IT WITH FLAGS

Semaphore, like most codes, is arbitrary. There is no
reason why a flag held out with the left hand should
mean "F", but everyone using the code knows that it
does. In the same way, the genetic code, by which DNA
is translated into protein, is arbitrary. The three
bases on DNA, cytosine-cytosine-guanine (in
that order), code for the amino acid proline
in a protein strand. Yet there is no
reason why they should code
for proline rather than
another amino acid.

Mammal

Scorpion

Fungus

E CODE FOR ALL

ery powerful piece of
dence for evolution is
fact that all living
igs – from insects
ungi, from humans to
ses – share the same genetic code
53). If there had been more than one
form originally, why should they all have
pted this same code, where each codon (three
A bases) has acquired a fixed but entirely arbitrary
ning? If, on the other hand, all life is descended from one
estor, this makes perfect sense. Once the code was established,
ould be very difficult for any changes in the code to evolve,
e these would undermine the whole system, making protein
duction impossible. Presumably, the code evolved at a very
y stage in the development of life. Fossil evidence suggests that
earliest forms were bacteria (p. 56), so it seems likely that they
ented" the genetic code now shared by all living things.

Sponge

Mollusc

The origin of life

How did life begin? Could it have originated from non-living matte by ordinary chemical processes? The earliest fossils are complex organ molecules 3,800 million years old. Before that there is no solid evidenc about the evolution of life, so scientists have to approach these questions in other ways. One approach is to try to recreate the conditions found on early Earth. Such experiments were first tried in tl 1950s and, to most people's surprise, they readily produced the sort of complex chemicals that are found only in living things. These include the building blocks of proteins, DNA and RNA (a molecule that is similar to DNA and is involved in protein production). If complex molecules such as these could have arisen spontaneously billions of years ago, why do they not still do so today? The answer is that conditions now are quite different. Most importantly, there is oxygen i the air, whereas there was almost none in Earth's atmosphere then. Once complex chemicals had formed on early Earth, several important steps would have been required before they became genuine living things. Some scientists believe that the first major step was the formation of an RNA molecule that could make exact copies of itself. Recently, small molecules of this kind have been made in the laboratory. A second major step was the development of a relationship between RNA and proteins and the establishment of a genetic code (p. 55).

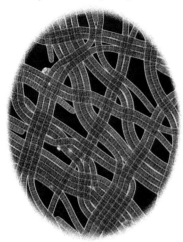

ENERGY INPUT
The chemicals found in living things are far more complex than those found in rocks or sea or air. To create complex molecules from simple ones, energy is required. One likely source of this energy on early Earth was lightning.

SELF-SUFFICIENCY BEGINS
The first bacteria must have lived by feeding on the complex chemicals still being produced, but in time they ate more than was being formed. When the supply ran short, many bacteria must have died out, but others, that could make their own food, evolved. These included the cyanobacteria, or blue-green algae (left).

THE OXYGEN REVOLUTION
Some bacteria use energy from the Sun to make their own food, as plants do, and in the process they release oxygen gas. When the first of these bacteria evolved, more than 3,500 million years ago, they began to produce oxygen, which slowly built up in the air. The oxygen combined with iron in the rocks to produce bands of ironstone (right) at this time. Oxygen changed the conditions on Earth so much that many creatures became extinct. In time, oxygen in the air also allowed new, larger, and more active animals to evolve. Such active life forms would have been impossible without oxygen.

**ST
TO**
Almos
living th
today are compose
cells. It is hard to
exactly when living th
became cellular. Some theorists sug
that the earliest life forms were "nak
RNA molecules, not surrounded by
membrane. Others believe th
membrane of some sort came
before RNA. They point out that cer
large molecules spontaneously fr
droplets, inside which other molec
could accumu

SEALED U
A cell is rather like a submar
The membrane of the
acts like the hull, crea
a sealed unit in which
internal conditions ca
closely controlled. C
certain substances
allowed to pass in or

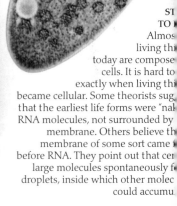

Electrical supply

Electrode

Tube through which gases circulate

Electrode

he dawn of life?

the early 1950s an American emist, Stanley Miller, devised periments to test ideas about e origin of life. He excluded all ygen from his apparatus and ed it with methane, monia, hydrogen, and ter vapour to simulate e atmosphere of ancient rth. Miller provided electrical spark to mic the flashes of htning that could ve provided a source energy. At the end the experiment, his paratus contained mplex molecules the kind of molecules und only in living ings. As yet, only e experimenter has anaged to persuade ese building blocks to n up spontaneously into nger and more complex olecules. Clearly, this was e next crucial step in the olution of life.

EDUCATED GUESSES
Stanley Miller, seen here at work in his laboratory, proposed that gases given off by volcanoes would have helped to create the atmosphere of ancient Earth. Other scientists agree with this, but some have disagreed about the exact gases present. They know that little oxygen was present and that there was probably water vapour in the air, but little else is certain. However, on the basis of educated guesses, several likely combinations of gases have been tried. Almost all of them have been found to produce the complex chemicals typical of living things.

Gas-filled reaction chamber

Inlet valve

Spark

Diagram of the apparatus used by Miller in his experiments

Vaporizing liquid

Condenser

Bunsen burner

Complex molecules collect here

Science and belief

MANY DIFFERENT CULTURES have traditional beliefs about how the living world was made (p. 6). These beliefs are not usually open to question or change. Scientific ideas about the history of life are different: the details of the story are continually changing because scientists work by looking for new evidence, by questioning existing theories and trying to develop better theories. In time, some theories become well established, and their basic points are accepted as fact simply because the evidence in their favour is overwhelming. The idea that the Earth goes round the Sun is one such theory. The idea that evolution has occurred is another. There may still be arguments over the details of how evolution occurred, but the fact that it did occur is not in doubt among scientists. One way of testing theories is to use them to make predictions and then to check those predictions. Because evolution proceeds so slowly, it is more difficult to test in this way than other scientific theories. (For the same reason, we do not normally notice evolution in action around us, even though it is continuing all the time.) Occasionally, however, evolutionary theories can be tested in the wild. A theory about how social insects evolved was used to make a prediction about evolution in mammals, and this was later confirmed by discoveries about the naked mole rat. Theories about natural selection were tested by observing the effects of cleaner air on the peppered moth.

APE OR ANGEL?
A 19th-century French cartoon shows Darwin in ape-like form, bursting through the hoops of credulity and ignorance held by the French physician and philosopher Maximilien Littré (1801–1881), a supporter of Darwin. The evidence that humans arose from ape-like ancestors by evolution is very strong (p. 63), but this idea troubles many people. Alfred Wallace (p. 36) solved his dilemma between science and belief by proposing that, while human beings had indeed evolved, the human spirit came from some supernatural source.

SCIENCE AND THE PRESS
Stephen Jay Gould (1941–2002) was among the scientists who continually tested and questioned the detail of evolution theory. Sadly newspapers often fail to understand this scientific process and assume that the whole idea of evolution is in doubt. They then report the scientific debates under dramatic and misleading headlines, such as the one below.

Darwin Wrong Scientist Claims

by our Science Correspondent

CLEANER AIR, PALER MOTHS
A dark form of the peppered moth replaced the paler form in industrial areas of England from the 1850s onwards. Scientists suspected that this was a result of pollution, reducing the camouflage of the pale moths (p. 36). Natural selection by moth-eating birds was thought to be at work. When, in the 1970s, laws were passed to reduce pollution, an unintentional "experiment" took place, allowing scientists to check their theory about why the darker form had taken over. In the next few years the air became cleaner. As predicted, the numbers of dark moths did fall, while the paler ones increased.

ON THE WRONG TRACK?
Could scientists be totally mistaken about evolution? This claim is sometimes made by opponents of the theory. However, in science, mistaken ideas do not survive for long, because theories are tested against experimental evidence. The case of Soviet geneticist Trofim Lysenko (1898–1976) proved this point. He favoured Lamarckian ideas (p. 13), since they agreed with Communist ideology, and he rose to power under Stalin. Lysenko banished Mendelian geneticists (p. 50), and dominated Soviet genetics for many years. Eventually, however, the evidence against Lamarckian inheritance was so strong that ideology had to give way to science. Lysenko was discredited and forced to resign.

Puzzle and prediction

Social insects, such as bees, wasps, and ants, live in colonies in which a single female produces all the offspring while the other members of the colony carry out duties of protection and feeding. How such social insects could have evolved has long been a puzzle. In the 1970s, the American zoologist Richard Alexander proposed an answer. He suggested that an insect species that cares for its young might evolve into a social insect as a direct result of living in a "fortress of food" – a well-defended nest to which food can be imported, or in which food is already available. He also made the bold prediction that a social mammal could evolve to live like these insects.

Naked mole rat hills formed during tunnelling

THE UNLIKELY MAMMAL

Alexander suggested that a mammal with a social life like a bee could have evolved. He predicted that if it did so, it would probably live in a place with a long dry season, where some plants have huge tubers. The mammal would be a burrower that could build its underground colony – its "fortress of food" – around these tubers. Several years later, to the amazement of scientists, South African zoologist Jennifer Jarvis revealed that the naked mole rat, an East African mammal, lives precisely as Richard Alexander had predicted.

Worker gathering food

WASP NEST

Wasps are social insects, like bees and termites. Each colony builds a complex nest, and at the centre of this nest, one female can remain safe and well fed. She produces all the young. The other wasps defend the colony or go out to collect food. Even if they are killed, their genes are passed on to the next generation, because the queen shares those genes. Until 1976, this odd way of life was known only among insects.

DIGGING BLINDLY

Like a worker wasp, the naked mole rat worker spends its time defending the colony, bringing food to the young, or tunnelling through the earth to find the tubers on which the colony feeds. While digging, it can close its mouth behind its front teeth, to avoid swallowing soil. It is almost blind, rarely venturing into daylight.

Naked mole rat queen in burrow

UNDERGROUND QUEEN

The queen is the only mole rat in the colony to produce offspring. She keeps the other females infertile by her dominant behaviour. She remains in the safety of the deepest part of the burrow (above) and is vigorously protected by the workers. In the nest chamber she suckles the young (right) until they are old enough to be fed on tubers by the workers.

Baby naked mole rats suckle at the queen's teats

DISPOSABLE WORKER

The workers live and die without producing any young. When the colony is under attack by a snake, workers may sacrifice their own lives in order to defend the colony, just as worker bees do.

Naked mole rat worker

The queen is larger than the workers

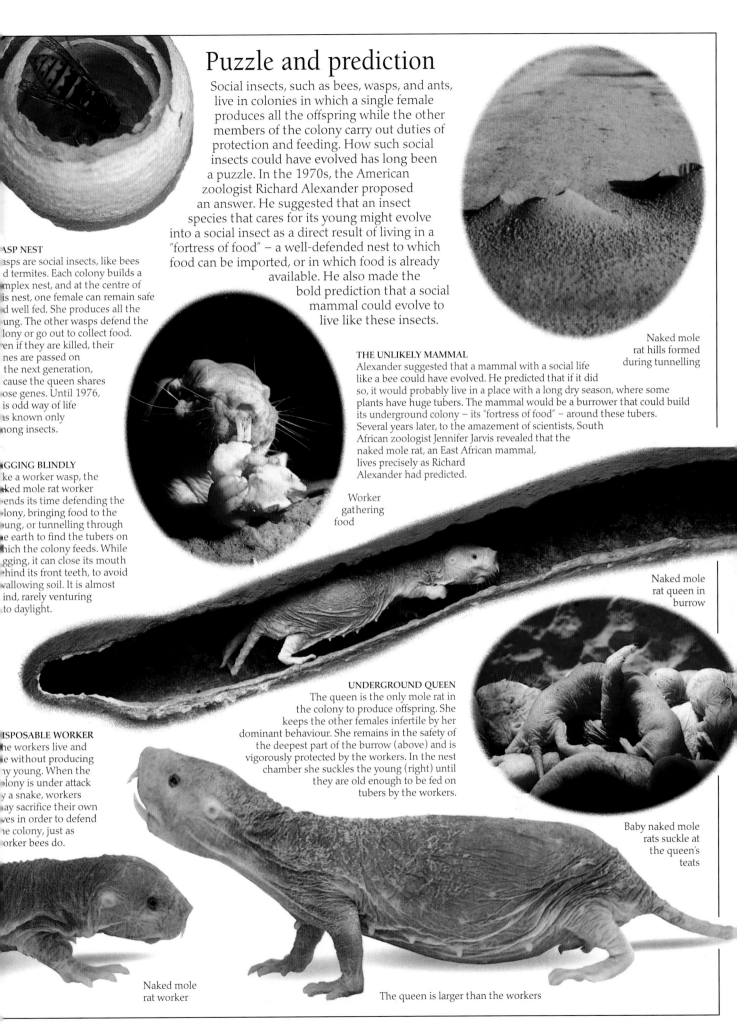

History of life

T̲HE SCIENTIFIC STUDY of rocks, fossils, and living things can be used to build up a picture of what happened in the past. Hundreds of scientists, working in different parts of the world, have helped to build up this picture. The details change as new evidence is constantly being found, and there are differences of opinion among scientists about some of the specific points. However, there is broad agreement on the major events, the general course of evolution, and the time-scale.

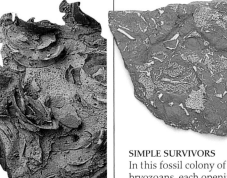

BEFORE LIFE
Meteorites were formed at the same time as Earth (p. 29). Earth's crust solidified 4,500 million years ago, but for millions of years Earth was empty of life. Although the early steps in the origin of life can only be guessed at (p. 56), the first fossils of bacteria are some 3,500 million years old.

BACTERIAL FOSSILS
Bacteria evolved into many types with different ways of obtaining their food. Some cyanobacteria (p. 56) form colonies that are large enough to be seen without the aid of a microscope.

GETTING LARGER
Only at the end of the Precambrian do readily visible, larger life forms appear. Most belong to the Ediacaran fauna (p. 47).

CAMBRIAN EXPLOSION
In the early Cambrian, many different kinds of complex marine animals suddenly appear in the fossil record.

BURGESS SHALE
Cambrian rocks reveal many different groups of invertebrate animals.

PLATE MOVEMENT
Over geological time, the movement of crustal plates has caused oceans to open and close and carried continents over Earth's surface.

Dry land

SIMPLE SURVIVORS
In this fossil colony of bryozoans, each opening contained a single tiny animal. Still found today, bryozoans have shown little change for millions of years, like many other simple creatures.

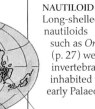

NAUTILOID
Long-shelled nautiloids such as *Orthoceras* (p. 27) were among the invertebrate animals that inhabited the seas of the early Palaeozoic era.

Shallow sea

SILURIAN SEAS
Primitive arthropods known as trilobites were abundant and widespread during the Ordovician and Silurian periods. Fossils of feeding tracks show that they lived on the sea floor. They later became extinct, as did the giant sea scorpions, large armoured animals up to 2 m (6 ft) long, with huge pincers.

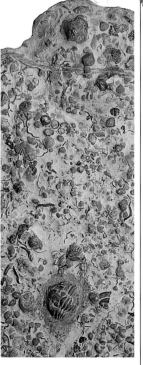

ARMOURED FISH
Many of the early jawless fish were covered in plates of bony armour, probably as a defence against the giant sea scorpions..

AGE OF FISH
During Devonian times some land masses were joined together to form large continents with vast dry regions and large rivers and lakes. With seasonal and dry climates, many water were prone to dry o These conditions favoured the surviva of groups of fish tha could breathe air an use their muscular f and limbs to move from one body of water to another.

PRECAMBRIAN	CAMBRIAN PERIOD	ORDOVICIAN PERIOD	SILURIAN PERIOD	DEVONIAN PERIOD
	PALAEOZOIC ERA			

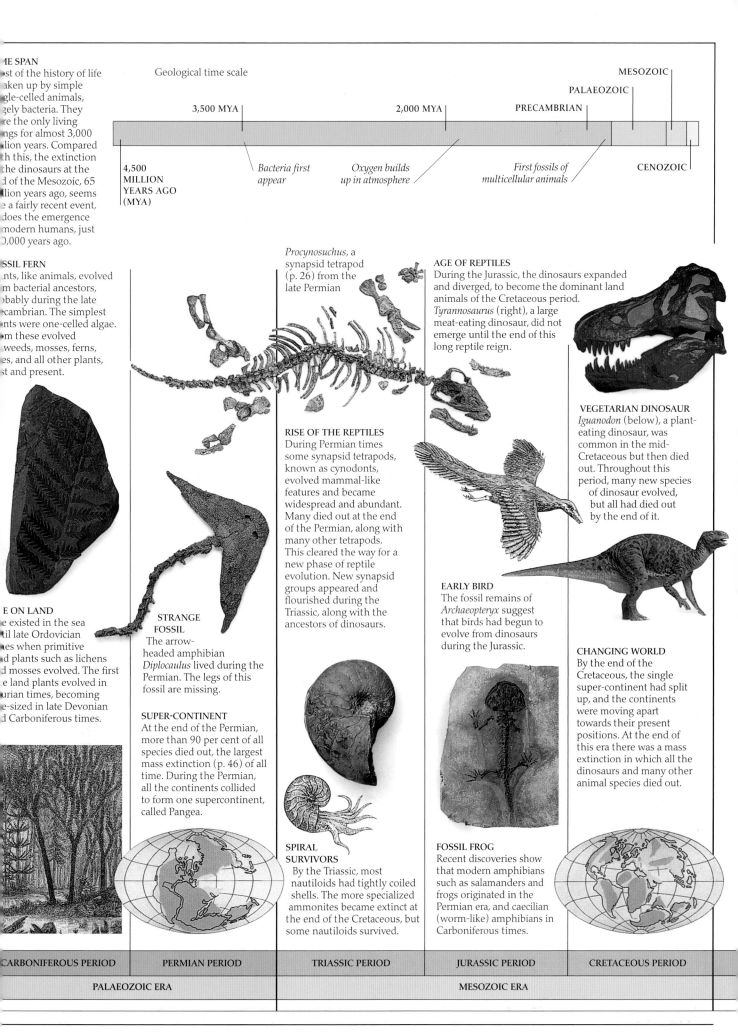

ME SPAN
st of the history of life
aken up by simple
gle-celled animals,
gely bacteria. They
re the only living
ngs for almost 3,000
lion years. Compared
th this, the extinction
the dinosaurs at the
d of the Mesozoic, 65
lion years ago, seems
e a fairly recent event,
does the emergence
modern humans, just
0,000 years ago.

SSIL FERN
nts, like animals, evolved
m bacterial ancestors,
bably during the late
cambrian. The simplest
nts were one-celled algae.
m these evolved
weeds, mosses, ferns,
es, and all other plants,
t and present.

E ON LAND
e existed in the sea
til late Ordovician
es when primitive
d plants such as lichens
d mosses evolved. The first
e land plants evolved in
urian times, becoming
e-sized in late Devonian
d Carboniferous times.

Geological time scale

3,500 MYA

2,000 MYA

PRECAMBRIAN

PALAEOZOIC

MESOZOIC

CENOZOIC

4,500
MILLION
YEARS AGO
(MYA)

Bacteria first appear

Oxygen builds up in atmosphere

First fossils of multicellular animals

Procynosuchus, a
synapsid tetrapod
(p. 26) from the
late Permian

STRANGE FOSSIL
The arrow-
headed amphibian
Diplocaulus lived during the
Permian. The legs of this
fossil are missing.

SUPER-CONTINENT
At the end of the Permian,
more than 90 per cent of all
species died out, the largest
mass extinction (p. 46) of all
time. During the Permian,
all the continents collided
to form one supercontinent,
called Pangea.

RISE OF THE REPTILES
During Permian times
some synapsid tetrapods,
known as cynodonts,
evolved mammal-like
features and became
widespread and abundant.
Many died out at the end
of the Permian, along with
many other tetrapods.
This cleared the way for a
new phase of reptile
evolution. New synapsid
groups appeared and
flourished during the
Triassic, along with the
ancestors of dinosaurs.

SPIRAL SURVIVORS
By the Triassic, most
nautiloids had tightly coiled
shells. The more specialized
ammonites became extinct at
the end of the Cretaceous, but
some nautiloids survived.

AGE OF REPTILES
During the Jurassic, the dinosaurs expanded
and diverged, to become the dominant land
animals of the Cretaceous period.
Tyrannosaurus (right), a
large meat-eating dinosaur, did not
emerge until the end of this
long reptile reign.

EARLY BIRD
The fossil remains of
Archaeopteryx suggest
that birds had begun to
evolve from dinosaurs
during the Jurassic.

FOSSIL FROG
Recent discoveries show
that modern amphibians
such as salamanders and
frogs originated in the
Permian era, and caecilian
(worm-like) amphibians in
Carboniferous times.

VEGETARIAN DINOSAUR
Iguanodon (below), a plant-
eating dinosaur, was
common in the mid-
Cretaceous but then died
out. Throughout this
period, many new species
of dinosaur evolved,
but all had died out
by the end of it.

CHANGING WORLD
By the end of the
Cretaceous, the single
super-continent had split
up, and the continents
were moving apart
towards their present
positions. At the end of
this era there was a mass
extinction in which all the
dinosaurs and many other
animal species died out.

CARBONIFEROUS PERIOD	PERMIAN PERIOD	TRIASSIC PERIOD	JURASSIC PERIOD	CRETACEOUS PERIOD
PALAEOZOIC ERA		MESOZOIC ERA		

Up to the present

F OR THE PAST 65 MILLION YEARS, mammals have been the dominant land animals. Their ancestors were small nocturnal creatures that evolved 200 million years ago from the synapsid tetrapods (p. 26). During the age of dinosaurs, they remained small but began to diversify with aquatic and gliding forms. Some preyed upon small dinosaurs. After the dinosaurs' extinction, mammals evolved rapidly, growing larger and more diverse. So too did the birds, but their bones are fragile, so there are relatively few in the fossil record.

ICE AGE BEAR
This cave bear skull is about 20,000 years old. These large bears lived during the last Ice Age and survived the extreme cold of winter by hibernating in cave. Mammals from the Quaternary period were more like present-day mammals than were those of the Tertiary, but many were far larger than their modern relatives.

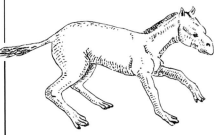

EARLY HORSE
Hyracotherium is one of the earliest horse-like mammals from 55 million years ago. The fact that evolution is not a steady march of progress is well illustrated by the horse (p. 48) and by mammal evolution in general. There has, however, been an increase in speed, intelligence, or size, in some mammal lines.

MIGHTY MASTODON
This vertebra (below) is from a mastodon (p. 14), an elephant-like animal that browsed on trees. The American mastodon survived into the Quaternary period and only died out about 10,000 years ago. Like many other large mammals that died out at this time, it may have fallen victim to human hunters.

SEAL FORERUNNER
Many of the early mammals were rather like dogs in shape and build. They gradually evolved into more specialized forms, such as seals, deer, and horses.

FISH AND PLANTS
It is not only the dominant animals (such as mammals) that continue to evolve, although this is the part of the story that attracts most interest. During the Cenozoic, there has been change among fish (above) and plants (left), as well as other living things.

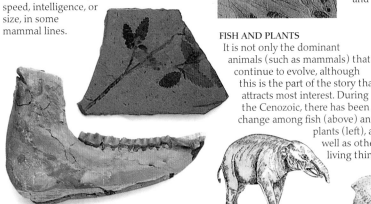

END OF THE LINE
The extinct *Palaeotherium* is known from this jaw and other fossils. It was a tapir-like animal.

EVOLUTIONARY ISLANDS
The separation of the continents affected mammal evolution greatly, with distinctive groups developing in isolated continents.

ALMOST AN ELEPHANT
The fossil known as *Phiomia* is part of the group that later gave rise to elephants, mammoths, and mastodons.

SABRE-TOOTH
Large tiger-like predators with massive stabbing teeth evolved to prey on slow-moving, thick-skinned creatures such as mammoths.

ANCIENT APE
Proconsul was an early ape that lived about 20 million years ago. Apes evolved from monkeys. They were very diverse 20 million years ago, but many died out as Earth's climate grew drier and the forests shrank.

ADVANCED LEAF
These leaves, which are about 20 million years old, are from a flowering plant, the most recent plant form to evolve. These only appeared during the Cretaceous. Until then the dominant plants were the conifers and cycads.

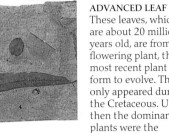

Fossil Miocene leaves

VANISHED BIRD
Moas, the giant birds of New Zealand (p. 25), show what might have happened in a world without mammals – birds could have become dominant. Early in the Tertiary period, when mammal were still all fairly small birds did in fact dominate. Huge flightless predatory birds evolved and preyed on mammals.

TERTIARY PERIOD

CENOZOIC ERA

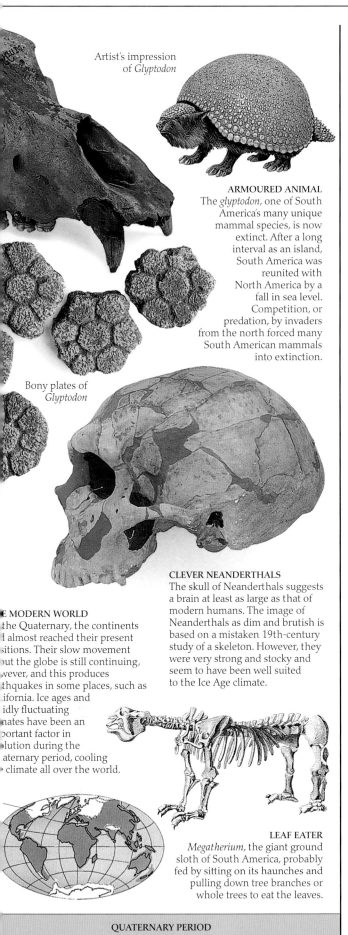

Artist's impression of *Glyptodon*

ARMOURED ANIMAL
The *glyptodon*, one of South America's many unique mammal species, is now extinct. After a long interval as an island, South America was reunited with North America by a fall in sea level. Competition, or predation, by invaders from the north forced many South American mammals into extinction.

Bony plates of *Glyptodon*

CLEVER NEANDERTHALS
The skull of Neanderthals suggests a brain at least as large as that of modern humans. The image of Neanderthals as dim and brutish is based on a mistaken 19th-century study of a skeleton. However, they were very strong and stocky and seem to have been well suited to the Ice Age climate.

E MODERN WORLD
the Quaternary, the continents almost reached their present sitions. Their slow movement ut the globe is still continuing, wever, and this produces thquakes in some places, such as ifornia. Ice ages and idly fluctuating nates have been an portant factor in lution during the aternary period, cooling climate all over the world.

LEAF EATER
Megatherium, the giant ground sloth of South America, probably fed by sitting on its haunches and pulling down tree branches or whole trees to eat the leaves.

QUATERNARY PERIOD

CENOZOIC ERA

Human evolution

The fossil record gives a clear picture of how upright-walking, large-brained creatures called hominids evolved from an ape-like ancestor. Fossil remains have been found of some 20 human-related species that have lived and died out over the last 6 million years since humans and chimps diverged. Few are represented by complete skeletons but they do indicate that small ape-like human relatives walked upright at least 4 million years ago before there was any significant increase in brain size which happened around 2.5 million years ago. The first members of our species (*Homo sapiens*) appeared in Africa some 200,000 years ago.

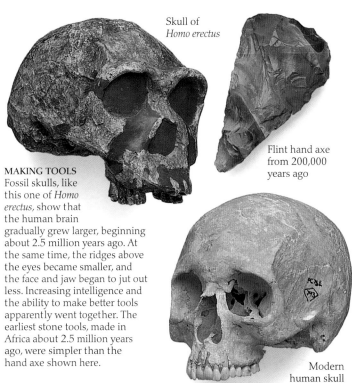

Skull of *Homo erectus*

Flint hand axe from 200,000 years ago

MAKING TOOLS
Fossil skulls, like this one of *Homo erectus*, show that the human brain gradually grew larger, beginning about 2.5 million years ago. At the same time, the ridges above the eyes became smaller, and the face and jaw began to jut out less. Increasing intelligence and the ability to make better tools apparently went together. The earliest stone tools, made in Africa about 2.5 million years ago, were simpler than the hand axe shown here.

Modern human skull

BIGGER BRAINS
Increasing intelligence undoubtedly contributed to the survival of early hominids. For example, *Homo erectus* cooperated to hunt large animals, and this would have required speech and intelligence. But the very great intelligence and creativity of modern humans seem to go beyond what might have aided survival in the wild. It is difficult to see musical gifts or mathematical abilities as a result of natural selection. Some human behaviour, good and bad, actually runs contrary to natural selection.

Mozart, the musical child prodigy

Classifying life

Taxonomy – the science of classifying organisms, both living and fossil – began with the work of Carl Linnaeus in the 18th century. Linnaeus set up a hierarchy of categories for grouping organisms with similar physical characteristics. Cladistics, or phylogenetics, is an alternative system developed in the 1950s and 1960s. It uses genetics, as well as physical characteristics, to sort organisms into groups called clades. From these, "family trees" are constructed to show the evolutionary development of species and the relationships between them.

CARL LINNAEUS
Linnaeus (1707–1778) was a Swedish botanist who studied and lectured at Uppsala University. Often referred to as the "father of taxonomy", he spent much of his life collecting, classifying, and naming plants and animals. In 1735, Linnaeus published the first edition of *Systema Naturae*, his classification of living organisms. Linnaeus's system – and his method of naming organisms – remains in use today.

Illustration from *Systema Naturae*

NAMING ORGANISMS
Linnaeus adopted Latin as the language of taxonomy. He gave each species a unique two-word name, or binomial, by combining its Latin genus and species names. For example, *Homo sapiens* is the binomial for modern humans. What makes the name unique is the species part. Extinct humans also carry the generic name *Homo*, such as *Homo habilis* ("handy man"), but only modern humans are referred to as *Homo sapiens* ("knowing man").

Fossil skull of *Homo habilis*

WHAT IS A SPECIES?
The basic unit of classification is the species. This is defined as a group of similar individuals that are capable of breeding together in the wild to produce fertile offspring (as opposed to infertile hybrids). For example, the Indian rhinoceros (*Rhinoceros unicornis*) cannot breed successfuly with any other of the five rhinoceros species, including the Javan rhinoceros (*Rhinoceros sondaicus*), the other one-horned species.

Indian rhinoceroses

LINNAEAN CLASSIFICATION
The kingdom, the largest grouping, is at the top of Linnaeus's classification hierarchy. There are five kingdoms, which separate living things into plants, fungi, animals, bacteria, and proctoctists. Each kingdom is divided into ever smaller categories. The smaller the category, the fewer the organisms in it and the more features they have in common. At the bottom of the hierarchy is the species – the most exclusive unit of classification, containing just one organism. The chart below shows the classification of the Indian rhinoceros.

KINGDOM: ANIMALIA
(Animals: 35 phyla).
The kingdom Animalia contains organisms that take food into their bodies and that develop from embryos.

PHYLUM: CHORDATA
(Chordates: 12 classes)
All animals in this phylum have a notocord – a precursor of the backbone – at some point in their lives.

CLASS: MAMMALIA
(Mammals: 28 orders)
Grouped in the class Mammalia are all animals that possess a single jawbone, fur, and mammary (milk-producing) glands.

ORDER: PERISSODACTYLA
(Odd-toed hoofed mammals: 3 families)
This is a group of plant-eating mammals that walk on odd-numbered toes. It includes horses, zebras, tapirs, and rhinoceroses.

FAMILY: RHINOCEROTIDAE
(Rhinoceroses: 5 genera)
This family within the Perissodactyla order contains the rhinoceroses – odd-toed hoofed mammals with horns on their noses.

GENUS: *RHINOCEROS*
(One-horned rhinoceroses: 2 species)
The genus *Rhinoceros* is made up of the one-horned rhinoceroses – the Indian and Javan rhinoceroses.

SPECIES: *UNICORNIS*
(Indian rhinoceros)
Found in Nepal, Bhutan, and India, this rhinoceros cannot breed with the smaller Javan rhinoceros, the other member of its genus.

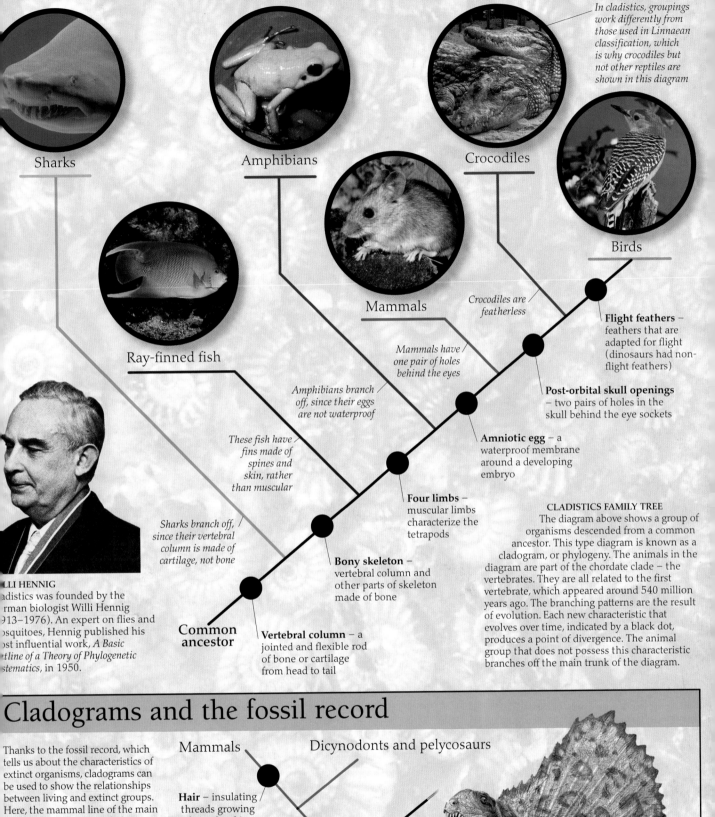

Sharks

Amphibians

Crocodiles

In cladistics, groupings work differently from those used in Linnaean classification, which is why crocodiles but not other reptiles are shown in this diagram

Birds

Mammals

Crocodiles are featherless

Ray-finned fish

Mammals have one pair of holes behind the eyes

Flight feathers – feathers that are adapted for flight (dinosaurs had non-flight feathers)

Amphibians branch off, since their eggs are not waterproof

Post-orbital skull openings – two pairs of holes in the skull behind the eye sockets

These fish have fins made of spines and skin, rather than muscular

Amniotic egg – a waterproof membrane around a developing embryo

Four limbs – muscular limbs characterize the tetrapods

Sharks branch off, since their vertebral column is made of cartilage, not bone

CLADISTICS FAMILY TREE
The diagram above shows a group of organisms descended from a common ancestor. This type diagram is known as a cladogram, or phylogeny. The animals in the diagram are part of the chordate clade – the vertebrates. They are all related to the first vertebrate, which appeared around 540 million years ago. The branching patterns are the result of evolution. Each new characteristic that evolves over time, indicated by a black dot, produces a point of divergence. The animal group that does not possess this characteristic branches off the main trunk of the diagram.

Bony skeleton – vertebral column and other parts of skeleton made of bone

WILLI HENNIG
...adistics was founded by the ...rman biologist Willi Hennig ...913–1976). An expert on flies and ...osquitoes, Hennig published his ...ost influential work, *A Basic ...tline of a Theory of Phylogenetic ...stematics*, in 1950.

Common ancestor

Vertebral column – a jointed and flexible rod of bone or cartilage from head to tail

Cladograms and the fossil record

Thanks to the fossil record, which tells us about the characteristics of extinct organisms, cladograms can be used to show the relationships between living and extinct groups. Here, the mammal line of the main diagram has been amended to include two extinct groups of mammal-like reptiles – dicynodonts and pelycosaurs. Like mammals, they developed in an amniotic egg and had a skull opening behind each eye (in humans this is reduced to an indentation). The development of hair separates the mammals from the dicynodonts and the pelycosaurs.

Mammals

Dicynodonts and pelycosaurs

Hair – insulating threads growing from the skin

Synapsid skull – a single and lower pair of skull openings behind the eyes

Amniotic egg – a waterproof membrane around a developing embryo

Dimetrodon, an extinct pelycosaur

Discoveries in evolution

OUR UNDERSTANDING OF LIFE AND ITS HISTORY has developed since Classical times, when scholars first questioned the nature of plants and animals, and their fossil remains. Hundreds of years of discoveries, especially those of the 19th and 20th centuries, increased our knowledge of the abundance, diversity, complexity, and evolution of life. Today, we understand the connections between the molecular and genetic make-up of a single cell and the whole of life and its evolution over 3.5 billion years.

c. 350–340 BCE
Aristotle, the ancient Greek naturalist, closely observes nature. He identifies around 560 different types of animal.

322 BCE
In Greece, Theophrastus, Aristotle's pupil, publishes *Historia Plantarum*, which classifies nearly 500 types of plant, and *De Causis Plantarum*, which explains plant growth.

c. 200 CE
Early Christian philosopher Tertullian asserts that fossils found on mountains were deposited there by the waters of the biblical flood. This idea is known as diluvialism.

1551
Conrad Gesner, a Swiss physician and naturalist, publishes *Historia Animalium*, a catalogue of the then known animals. He follows this in 1565 with *De Rerum Fossilium* ("On Things Dug Out of the Earth"), which is one of the first illustrated catalogues of fossils.

1673
Antoni van Leeuwenhoek, a Dutch draper and amateur naturalist, uses a microscope to reveal details of animal and plant cells for the first time. His microscope can magnify objects 250 times.

1694
Rudolph Jakob Camerarius, a German professor of physics at the University of Tubingen, publishes his *Epistola de Sexu Plantarium*. He includes experimental evidence to show that plants reproduce sexually with the deposit of male pollen on the female stigma.

Hibiscus rosa-sinensis flower, showing a long stigma

Stigma

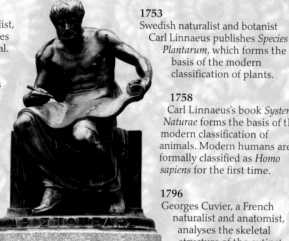
Statue of Aristotle

1753
Swedish naturalist and botanist Carl Linnaeus publishes *Species Plantarum*, which forms the basis of the modern classification of plants.

1758
Carl Linnaeus's book *Systema Naturae* forms the basis of the modern classification of animals. Modern humans are formally classified as *Homo sapiens* for the first time.

1796
Georges Cuvier, a French naturalist and anatomist, analyses the skeletal structure of the extinct *Megatherium* from an illustration, and concludes that it had been a giant ground sloth. Cuvier's work shows how all vertebrates have a common basic skeletal structure, whose modifications give clues to how each animal lives.

Fossilized claw of *Megatherium*

1801
American showman Charles Wilson Peale excavates the skeleton of a mastodon, an extinct relative of the elephant.

1802
English clergyman William Paley publishes *Natural Theology, or Evidence of the Existence and Attributes of the Deity*, which views all adaptation in the natural world as evidence of God's handiwork.

1809
The publication of a treatise *Philosophie Zoologie* by French naturalist Jean-Baptiste de Lamarck, gives the first reasoned theory of "transformism", which we now know as evolution.

1822
British doctor and fossil hunter Gideon Man discovers teeth from an extinct giant reptile he names *Iguanodon*.

1826
German biologist Karl Ernst von Baer discov the egg cells in female mammals. This lays th foundation of modern embryology, describir embryonic development from egg stage to bi

1830–1833
Charles Lyell, a British geologist, publishes h *Principles of Geology*, which argues that the distant past should be explored only through understanding of the natural forces operating the present. This becomes known as the principle of uniformitarianism.

1832–1836
HMS *Beagle* makes a round-the-world survey voyage under Captain Robert Fitzroy, with English naturalist Charles Darwin invited as the expedition's naturalist.

1837
Charles Darwin begins a notebook on the "transmutation" of species.

19th-century dinosaur illustration

1841
British anatomist Richard Owen coins the name dinosaur ("terrible lizard"), and publishe the first description of the dinosaurs' defining characteristics.

1844
The anonymously published book *Vestiges of the Natural History of Creation* outlines a theo for the evolution of life from primitive single celled organisms to more complex, advanced forms such as humans. In 1884, it is finally revealed that the book was written by the Scottish publisher Robert Chambers.

1844
Charles Darwin shows an outline of his theory of evolution to the British botanist Joseph Hooker.

1854
Alfred Wallace, a British naturalist and professional collector, independently comes u with the idea of evolution by natural selection while working in Malaysia and Indonesia.

1858
Charles Darwin and Alfred Wallace produce a short joint paper on evolution by natural selection. Its publication is arranged by Joseph Hooker and Charles Lyell.

1859
Charles Darwin publishes his book *On the Origi of Species*, which outlines his ideas on evolutio

ish biologist Thomas Henry Huxley defends
win's theory of evolution at the Oxford
ting of the British Association for the
ancement of Science, when it is attacked by
Bishop of Oxford, Samuel Wilberforce.

Model of
Archaeopteryx

1
Germany, a fossil of *Archaeopteryx*, a primitive
d, is found. It has impressions of feathers and
ng, bony tail. Huxley realizes that this fossil
ks birds and reptiles, making it the first good
dence to support Darwin's theory of evolution.

53
e first extinct human relative (*Homo
nderthalensis*) is described and named by
liam King, a geology professor in Galway,
land. The fossil remains had been found in
rmany in 1856, but were not at first thought
be different from modern humans.

66
strian monk Gregor Mendel publishes an
count of his experiments with breeding
a plants. He realizes that peas carry "particles"
heredity (now called genes), some of which
more dominant than others.

66
tish physicist William Thomson, later Lord
lvin, says that Earth is 100 million years old
most – not the many hundreds of millions of
ars suggested by Darwin and Lyell. In fact,
th is about 4,500 million years old – closer
Darwin and Lyell's estimate than Thomson's.

70s
nst Haeckel, a German biologist and
turalist, develops the idea of "evolution as
ogress", which assumes that all nature is
oving towards a final goal: human beings.

07
merican geneticist Thomas Hunt Morgan
gins his work on fruit flies. His research
ll help to show that most characteristics are
ntrolled by many genes (tiny stretches of
e molecule DNA).

1930
English mathematician Ronald Fisher publishes
The Genetical Theory of Natural Selection.
It proves that Mendel's ideas on genetics
support Darwin's theory of natural selection,
rather than oppose it, as was previously thought.

1953
The double-helix structure of the DNA
molecule is published by American James
Watson and Englishman Francis Crick.

1962
American scientists Linus Pauling and
Emile Zuckerkandl develop the idea of the
molecular clock. This uses differences in DNA
sequences and proteins between species to
calculate how long ago two species diverged.

1968
American geneticist Sewell Wright
publishes the first volume of his
treatise on *Evolution and the
Genetics of Populations*. He
uses mathematics to link
genetics to natural selection,
and develops the idea of
genetic drift – that random
changes can occur in genes
by chance, rather than by
natural selection.

1968
Japanese geneticist
Motoo Kimura proposes
his neutral theory of
molecular evolution,
which states that genetic
changes can occur at the
molecular level that have
no influence on an
individual's fitness.

Dolly the cloned sheep,
1996

1996
British biologists Ian Wilmut and Keith
Campbell clone (reproduce) a lamb called Dolly
from a single adult udder cell of a black-faced
ewe. Dolly is an exact genetic copy of that ewe,
instead of having inherited her genes from two
genetically different parents. Scientists think
that cloning can help genetic research, but some
people see it as tampering with nature.

The mouse
genome was
outlined in
2002

2000
The working draft of the international Human
Genome Project is published. The project aims
to find the make-up of the human genome –
the sequence of base pairs that make up human
DNA and the 25,000 or so human genes. The
project began in 1990, headed by James Watson.

2002
The mouse genome is outlined. Of the mouse's
30,000 or so genes, some 80 per cent have
direct counterparts in the human genome,
and 99 per cent show some similarity.

2003
The complete draft of the human
genome is published. Further
analysis continues.

2005
Publication of the outline of
chimp genome, which is only
2.7 per cent different from
the human genome. These
differences, which include
certain genes involved in
speech development, have
evolved over the 6 million
years or so since humans
and chimps last shared a
common ancestor.

2006
The Neanderthal Genome Project
is announced by Germany's Max
Planck Institute. It is already known that
Neanderthal and human DNA is 99.5 per cent
identical, and that the genomes are roughly the
same size. Ancient DNA from a 38,000-year-old
male Neanderthal from Croatia is currently
being extracted and sequenced to produce an
outline of the Neanderthal genome.

Human genome research, 1990 to present

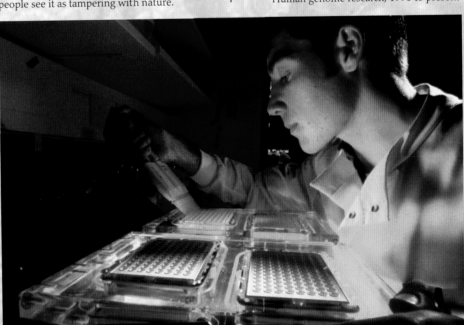

Find out more

THE SCIENTIFIC STUDY OF EVOLUTION is over 150 years old. Since Darwin and Wallace first proposed their theory in 1858, a vast amount has been published by scientists on the subject. Never before has there been so much information available about evolution and related topics such as fossils, natural history, and the protection and conservation of wildlife. You can find facts, figures, and stories in public libraries and on the Internet, get a feel for the stunning variety of animal life at a zoo, and encounter the creatures of the past in a museum. You can also get involved by joining a conservation group or taking up a nature hobby.

Field Museum, Chicago, Illinois

Meeting the animals at Singapore Zoo

ZOOS AND BOTANICAL GARDENS
The world's major zoos and botanical gardens allow to appreciate life's diversity and abundance, and get close to the extraordinary animals and plants that populate our planet. Today, zoos and botanical gardens also play a vital role in the conservation of rare and endangered species, reminding us of how we relate to and affect the natural world around us.

USEFUL WEBSITES

- Understanding Evolution, a website from the Museum of Paleontology, California, is an excellent in-depth interactive site on evolution: **http://evolution.berkeley.edu**
- The American Museum of Natural History has an outstanding natural history and evolution site; its "Ology" section is specially for kids: **www.amnh.org**
- The website of the USA's Smithsonian Institution has an "Explore a topic" link with resources on subjects such as "The Evolving Earth" and "The Diversity of Life": **www.mnh.si.edu**
- London's Natural History Museum website has a "Kids only" section that includes an illustrated directory of 325 different dinosaurs: **www.nhm.ac.uk**
- Discovering Fossils is packed with details on how and where to look for fossils in the UK, plus information on equipment and safety: **www.discoveringfossils.co.uk**
- The World Wildlife Fund's website has databases, photo galleries, video clips, images from camera traps, games, and more: **www.wwf.org**
- The BBC's Science and Nature website has natural history news, plus links on UK wildlife, conservation, fossils, dinosaurs, human origins, and evolution for children: **www.bbc.co.uk/sn/**
- The IUCN's Red List (see opposite) has a searchable website with information on species facing a high risk of global extinction: **www.iucnredlist.org**

VISIT A MUSEUM
A visit to a natural history museum is a great way to get a good overview of the development of life on Earth, and the weird and wonderful species that populated the planet in past ages. Many museums have interactive displays and some exhibit spectacular dinosaur skeletons. Most museums maintain their own websites that give opening times and background information on the objects in their collections.

...URE HOBBIES

...n childhood, Charles Darwin was a keen collector
...ugs. A hands-on nature hobby, such as bird-
...hing, bug hunting, or plant identification, is still
... way of getting to know how nature works.
...ng photos and making notes and drawings will
... you learn to identify different species. If you do
...ct animal specimens, make sure you return them
...eir natural habitats.
... plants should be
...erved rather
... picked.

Using a net is an easy way to catch flying insects, but they should always be released again once you have studied them

Places to visit

AMERICAN MUSEUM OF NATURAL HISTORY, NEW YORK, USA
The museum has the world's single largest collection of dinosaur fossils, with over 100 specimens on show. Pay them a visit at night, on one of the museum's sleepovers!

MUSEUM VICTORIA, MELBOURNE, AUSTRALIA
The museum's Discovery Centre and Education Program provide a wide range of exhibits and materials relating to natural history.

NATURAL HISTORY MUSEUM, LONDON
Highlights of this world-famous museum include a *Diplodocus* skeleton, an animated *Tyrannosaurus*, a life-size blue whale model, and a 1,300-year-old giant sequoia tree.

THE SMITHSONIAN INSTITUTION, WASHINGTON, DC, USA
The stunning new Sant Ocean Hall lets you explore the ocean, from the sunlit surface to the dark depths, from prehistory to today, and from the smallest microorganisms to the largest animals ever known.

Conservation work on a reed bed

Bivalve

Brachiopod

Drawer with fossil specimens

COLLECTING FOSSILS
Fossils provide important and fascinating evidence for evolution. Fossil collecting is a hobby that can be enjoyed by anyone, but it is essential to check whether it is legal to collect from a particular site, since many countries have strict rules about collecting and you may need a licence. Always make sure you are supervised by an adult when you are fossil collecting, and use the correct equipment, such as rock hammers, safety helmets, goggles, and gloves. Never collect below cliffs or anywhere there might be rockfalls.

Coral

Echinoid

Ammonite

...CAL CONSERVATION GROUPS
...ery region has its own natural history heritage.
...ere is now a growing appreciation of how
...uable, and how fragile, this heritage is. Many
...nservation groups work to protect local
...dlife and its habitats, and the fossil sites that
... us about life in the past. Most groups
...ganize days when you can take an active part
...conservation by helping with tasks such as
...aring scrub, replanting, and so on. Public
...raries and web-based searches can provide
...mes and addresses of local groups.

INTERNATIONAL CONSERVATION
Your school class could fund-raise and campaign for international organizations like the World Wildlife Fund, which promotes the cause of wildlife conservation worldwide. The International Union for the Conservation of Nature (IUCN) is a global body that works to find solutions to problems that put species at risk. Its Red List gives the current status of plant and animal species that are threatened with extinction. It is updated regularly.

Conservation workers help a cheetah in Africa

Glossary

ACQUIRED CHARACTERISTICS The non-inheritable characteristics acquired by an organism in its lifetime. Large muscles produced by weight-lifting are acquired characteristics.

ADAPTATION The process of modification by natural selection that makes an organism more able to survive and reproduce in its environment. Also, any characteristic produced by this process.

ALLELE One of two or more alternative forms of the same gene.

AMINO ACID One of a group of 20 carbon-based molecules that form the building blocks of thousands of different proteins in living things.

ARTIFICIAL SELECTION The alteration of a population of plants or animals by selective breeding carried out by humans. Dog breeds, for example, are produced by artificial selection.

BASE A chemical compound that forms part of a DNA molecule. Bases form the "rungs" of the molecule's ladder-like structure, with two bases (a base pair) per rung.

BINOMIAL The two-word scientific name of an organism, made up of its Latin genus and species names. The binomial of modern humans, for example, is *Homo sapiens*.

CAMBRIAN EXPLOSION The emergence of many new and complex life forms in the Cambrian Period (542–488 million years ago).

CATASTROPHE THEORY The 19th-century idea that the change in fossils from rocks of one geological period to the next could be explained by global catastrophes such as great floods, powerful earthquakes, or changes in climate.

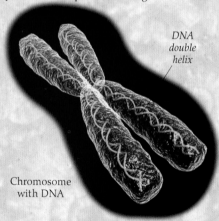

DNA double helix

Chromosome with DNA

CELL A tiny unit of living matter. Cells are the building blocks of all living things. The control centre of a cell is the nucleus.

CHROMOSOMES Thread-like DNA packages found in the cell nucleus. They carry genes and all the information needed to make a cell work.

CLADISTICS A method of classification in which members of a group, or clade, share a more recent common ancestor with one another than with members of any other group. Cladistics is also known as phylogenetics.

CLADOGRAM A branching diagram, or phylogeny, showing the evolutionary history and inter-relationship of species.

CLONE To produce a genetic replica of a cell or organism; also, the replica itself. Cloning occurs in organisms that reproduce from a single parent (asexual reproduction). Scientists have succeeded in cloning organisms artificially in the laboratory.

COMMON ANCESTOR An ancestral species shared by two or more species. Modern humans and chimps share a common ancestor that lived at least six million years ago.

COMPETITION The struggle between organisms for limited resources, leading to natural selection.

DARWINISM The original theory proposed by Darwin that species evolve from other species by natural selection. Neo-Darwinism is modified by the addition of Mendelism, of which Darwin was not aware.

DILUVIALISM The mistaken idea that all rock strata and fossils were laid down at the same time by catastrophic flooding.

DINOSAURS An extinct group of land-dwelling reptiles that lived in the Mesozoic Era (251–65 million years ago).

DNA Short for deoxyribonucleic acid, which is present in every cell and which gives the hereditary characteristics to a parent organism.

DOMINANT GENE A gene (allele) that shows itself in a living organism's phenotype, or physical form. In humans, the gene for brown eyes is dominant over the gene for blue eyes.

DOUBLE HELIX The coiled, twisted ladder shape of the DNA molecule.

EMBRYO An unborn living organism at an early stage of development.

ENZYME A protein that speeds up and regulates chemical reactions.

EVOLUTION Changes in the genetics and forms of organisms over time.

EXTINCTION The natural dying out of species.

FOSSIL The preserved trace of a once-living organism. Fossils are usually bodily remains (bones, teeth, or shells), footprints, dung, or the impressions of body features.

FOSSILIZATION The way that the buried remains of organisms are preserved when the sediment around them is transformed into r...

GENE A stretch of DNA that carries instruct... to make a particular protein. Genes are the basic units of heredity, which are passed on to the next generation.

Euoplocephal... dinosau...

GENETIC CODE The arrangement of bases in a DNA molecule. The genetic code tells a cell h... to convert the sequence of bases into a seque... of amino acids, from which proteins can be b...

GENETIC DRIFT Randomly occurring char... in the genetic make-up of a population, occur... at the molecular level, rather than by selecti...

GENOME All the DNA in a cell or organism...

GENOTYPE The genetic information that an organism inherits from its parents. The genotype interacts with the environment to produce the organism's phenotype.

GENUS A category of classification containi... one or more closely related species.

GEOLOGICAL PERIOD A unit of time represented by a sequence of rock strata and their characteristic fossils. Geological periods are subdivided into epochs and stage... and grouped into eras.

Fossilized frog

Mule – a hybrid of a donkey and a horse

MOLECULE A tiny particle of a chemical substance. Molecules are made up of even smaller particles called atoms.

MUTATION A change in a cell's genetic material. If a mutation occurs in a reproductive cell, it can be passed on from one generation to another.

NATURAL SELECTION The process by which organisms that are poorly suited to their environment are slowly weeded out because they fail to survive. Those that are fitter and well adapted to their environment survive better, and produce more offspring. As a result, they pass on their genes to future generations.

NATURAL THEOLOGY The idea that the adaptation of organisms to their surroundings is evidence of design by a creator God.

PHENOTYPE The physical characteristics of an organism that result from the interaction between its genotype and the environment.

PLATE TECTONICS The slow movement of the solid rocky plates of Earth's outer layer, or crust, as new sea-floor rocks are generated and older sea-floor rocks are recycled.

PROTEIN A chain-like molecule made up of amino acids. Proteins form the organic (carbon-based) compounds that are characteristic of living things.

RECAPITULATION The mistaken 19th-century idea that as an embryo develops it goes through all the evolutionary stages of its ancestors.

Migrating monarch butterflies

RECESSIVE GENE A gene (allele) that is hidden when it is partnered by a dominant gene. It only shows in the phenotype if it is partnered by an identical recessive gene. In humans, the gene for red hair is recessive.

RNA (Ribonucleic acid) RNA is a molecule similar to DNA. It is present in all organisms, and translates the genetic code into proteins.

SEDIMENTARY ROCK A type of rock formed from the debris of other rocks and sometimes the remains of living organisms.

SEXUAL SELECTION A type of selection in which individuals are favoured (selected) over others of the same sex because of their mating behaviour. Examples include males fighting for access to females, and females choosing males on the basis of their courtship displays.

Courtship display in ducks

SPECIES A group of organisms that can breed together in the wild. Also a basic unit of classification, referred to by its Latin binomial.

SPONTANEOUS GENERATION The false notion that new microorganisms spontaneously arise from non-living matter, such as wet straw.

SUBSPECIES A group within a species that has recognizable characteristics, often geographically separated from the rest of the species so that interbreeding is not possible. This is often the first step in the formation of a new species.

TAXONOMY The science of classifying and naming living and extinct organisms.

TETRAPOD An vertebrate with four limbs, or an animal that has evolved from one.

UNIFORMITARIANISM The 19th-century idea that the past can be understood only in relation to the natural forces operating in the present.

VARIATION The naturally occurring differences between individuals and populations of the same species that have a genetic basis, such as colour and pattern variations on the shells of seashore molluscs.

VERTEBRATE An animal with a backbone, or spine. The individual bones of the spine are known as vertebrae.

[HE]REDITY The [gen]etic link between [suc]cessive generations [of] living organisms.

[H]OMINID One of a group [of] upright-walking, large-[bra]ined mammals that evolved [fro]m ape-like ancestors. [Hu]mans are hominids.

[HY]BRID The offspring of a [cro]ss between two separate but [rel]ated species. Hybrids are [inf]ertile, and cannot reproduce.

[IC]E AGE An extremely cold [pe]riod in Earth's history, when the ice [sh]eets were much larger than they are today.

[IN]HERITANCE The passing on of [ch]aracteristics from generation to generation.

[IN]TERBREEDING Sexual reproduction [be]tween organisms that involves the exchange [of] reproductive cells and their DNA.

Invertebrate worm

[IN]TERMEDIATE A living or fossil species that [re]presents an "in-between" stage or link in the [ev]olution of a new group from an existing one.

[IN]VERTEBRATE An animal lacking a backbone.

[IS]OLATING MECHANISM Scents, sounds, [co]lours, and behavioural signals used by a species [to] recognize its own kind for breeding.

[L]AMARCKISM A mistaken theory proposed [by] Jean-Baptiste Lamarck that an individual can [in]herit characteristics acquired by its parents [du]ring their lifetime.

[L]OCUS The position of particular [ge]ne on a chromosome.

[M]ASS EXTINCTION Rare, relatively [br]ief catastrophic events that cause a [si]gnificant percentage of organisms on [E]arth to die out.

[M]ENDELISM The rules governing the [w]ay that individual characteristics are [pa]ssed from parent organisms to their [off]spring via dominant, recessive, and [s]ex-linked genes.

[M]IGRATION The movement of organisms [fr]om one place to another, either as individuals, [g]roups, or whole populations. If this results in [th]e organisms becoming isolated from the [r]est of their species, they may eventually [e]volve into a new species.

Index

Acknowledgements

Dorling Kindersley would like to thank:
Jeremy Adams, John Cooper and Gerald Legg at the Booth Museum, Hove; Solene Morris at Down House; Nick Arnold, Ian Bishop, David Carter, Sandra Chapman, Paul Clark, Andy Currant, Paul Hillyard, Jerry Hooker, Robert Kruszynski, David Lewis, Tim Parmenter, Alison Paul, David Reid, Lee Rogers and Sally Young at the Natural History Museum; Denise Blagden; Tom Kemp, Philip Powell, Monica Price and Derek Siveter at the Oxford University Museum; and Jack Challoner, for all their advice and help with the provision of objects for photography; Margaret Brown of the Medical Research Council, Cambridge; Chris Faulkes of the Institute of Zoology, London; and Jim Hamill at the British Museum (Ethnographic), for their help; Sarah Ashun, Jonathan Buckley, Jane Burton, Peter Chadwick, Philip Dowell, Andreas von Einsiedel, Frank Greenaway, Derek Hall, Colin Keates, Dave King, Karl Shone and Jerry Young for photography; Deborah Rhodes for page make-up. **DTP Manager** Joanna Figg-Latham. **Illustrations** Stephen Bull and Frazer May. **Index** Jane Parker.

Publisher's note No animal has been injured or harmed in any way during the preparation of this book.

For this edition, the publisher would also like to thank: consultant Kim Bryan for assisting

with the updates; Lisa Stock for editorial assistance, David Ekholm-JAlbum, Sunita Gahir, Susan Malyan, Susan St Louis, Lisa Stock and Bulent Yusuf for the clipart; Sue Nicholson and Edward Kinsey for the wallchart; Monica Byles and Stewart J Wild for proofreading.

Picture credits

The publisher would like to thank the following for their kind permission to reproduce their photographs:

(Key: a-above; b-below/bottom; c-centre; f-far; l-left; r-right; t-top)

Alamy Images: blickwinkel / S. Gerth 71cra; David R. Frazier Photolibrary, Inc. 68l; The London Art Archive 64cla; Mary Evans Picture Library 66cr; PHOTOTAKE Inc. 67cra; Nick Turner 69clb. **American Museum of Natural History:** 65cl. **American Philosophical Society, Philadelphia:** 15bl. **Ancient Art and Architecture Collection:** 8br, 16br. **Bettmann Archive:** 50bl, 57bl. **The Bridgeman Art Library:** 20bl; Natural History Museum, London 64c. **British Library:** 7bl, 7bc. **British Museum:** 16bl. **Neil Bromhall:** 59cr; 59cl. **Brown Brothers:** 41br. **Camera Press:** 52bl, 58tr. **Bruce Coleman:** Stephen Bord 11 tr, 35tl; Pekka Hallor 39br, 43br; Hans Rheinart

53br; Konrad Wothe 47cr. **Corbis:** Dung Vo Trung / Politika 69bc. **DK Images:** Josef Hlasek 65cra (wood mouse); Mike Linley 65tc; Natural History Museum, London 64clb, 64-71 (background), 66cb, 69crb; Rough Guides 65tl, 68tr. **Chris Faulkes:** 59tr. **Getty Images:** Joseph Van Os / The Image Bank 71bc. **Giraudon:** 40tl. **Michael Holford:** 6bc, 30bl. **Hulton Deutsche Collection Ltd:** 13tr, 13cr, 17cr, 21cl, 28tl, 36bc, 43tr, 54cr. **Illustrated London News Picture Library:** 30cr. **Mansell Collection:** 12tl, 14tl, 17tl, 19bl, 20cl, 21cr, 29tr, 33cl, 34tr, 36tl, 41cl, 42cl, 63br. **Mary Evans Picture Library:** 9bl, 10tl, 13br, 19cl, 25bc, 42-3c, 48cr, 56br, 61bl. **Professor Rory Mortimore, University of Brighton:** 11 cr. MRC Laboratory of Molecular Biology: 53l. **Natural History Museum Picture Library:** 12cr, 18cr, 19tl, 24br, 25tc. **N.H.P.A.:** 38br; Philippa Scott 39cr, 42bl. **Oxford Scientific Films:** 35tr, 36cr. **Peale Museum, Baltimore:** 15cl. **Pennsylvania Academy of Fine Arts:** 14tr. **Planet Earth / Richard Coomber:** 39cl, 47tr. **Ann Ronan at Image Select:** 10bl, 50tl. **Department of Palaeontology, Royal Belgian Institute of Natural Sciences, Brussels:** 19tr. **Royal Society:** 19ct, 24tl, 29tl. **Science Museum Photo Library:** 7tr; Jean-Loup Charmet 16tl, 17bl, 29cl; Eric Grave 56cl; James King-Holmes 67br; NASA 29bc, 46cr, 50c, 50cb, 50br, 52cl, 58tl; Novosti 58bl; David Parker 54tl; Pasieka 70clb; Sinclair Stammers 56cr. **St Paul's Girls School:** 52tl. **By permission of the Syndics of Cambridge**

University Library: 30cl.Transylvania University Library, Special Collections, Kentucky: 22tl. **Werner Foreman Archive:** 7tl. **Professor H. B. Whittington, University of Cambridge:** 46tl, 47tl, 60bl. **William Sturgis Bigelow Collection, Museum of Fine Arts, Boston:** 6tr. **Zefa:** 37cl, 49tr, 56tl.

Wallchart
DK Images: Booth Museum of Natural History, Brighton c (all butterflies, except 1st from right, 1st row), clb (grasshopper, stick insects and cockroach); The Home of Charles Darwin, Down House (English Heritage) / Natural History Museum, London cl (telescope and compass); Natural History Museum, London bc (flint hand axe), bl (skulls), br, ftr; Getty Images: fcla.

All other images © Dorling Kindersley
For further information see:
www.dkimages.com